Be the Inspiration:
7 Ways to Inspire Your World

Sheri Kaye Hoff

DEDICATION

*For all of you who are committed to not only
becoming inspired, but to being the inspiration
every day for everyone around you*

CONTENTS

ACKNOWLEDGMENTS

Thank you to these people and organizations who have inspired me while writing this book.

My family, Randy, Monikka, Sonja, Nicholas, Cassie, Chris, Jeff, Connie Nylund, John Nylund , Brita Sorenson, Marci Shimoff, Hasmark Services, Hay House, Crystal Andrus, Crystal Miller, Janet Nestor, Eva Gregory, Maria Erving, Mary Allen, Nancy Farris, Christy Calbos, Linda Hardenstein, Dr Joe Rubino, Michele Caron, Doug Jarvie, Nancy Falconi, Chantal Beaupre, Vimala Murali, Norma Schaffer, Kathryn Quintana, Hemal Radia, Erin Ruiz, Bonnie Gortler, Pat Hastings, Nanice Ellis, Tomar Levine, Cari Murphy, Lena Salonikas, Jeanna Gabellini, Stephen Covey, Viktor Frankl, Catherine Ponder, Esther and Jerry Hicks, Suze Orman, Louise L. Hay, all of my clients, Success Club members, coaching groups, and all of my Your Path to Success Telesummit guests and attendees.

CHAPTER 1: INTRODUCTION

"You make a living by what you get. You make a life by what you give." - **Winston Churchill**

Do you feel a pull to do and be more?

Is it important to you to be able to inspire yourself and those around you?

Do you want to be more effective and impactful in your career or business?

Does your level of personal and team leadership influence your income?

It is important to be inspired, to feed our souls on a daily basis. Once you become adept at knowing what inspires you personally, then the next natural move is to inspire the world around you. This is the time when you help others transform through your message, your example.

Ask yourself, what can I teach? How can I lead? How can I inspire? Who can I inspire? This is a time for mentoring and giving back. You do have something that is uniquely you... that can help those around you... your job is to find out what that is and make a commitment to truly BE the Inspiration.

This book- *BE the Inspiration: 7 Ways to Inspire Your World* is designed to take you from getting inspired personally to becoming the inspiration to those around you. Learn what it takes to become an inspiring leader so you can grow your business, become a leader in your profession, lead a program, make a difference and/or become a thought leader. Learn how to use your personal development story to create a meaningful and inspiring platform.

Through the use of the acronym INSPIRE, you will learn key components of explosive personal and leadership growth.

What do I mean when I say- "Be the inspiration"?

There is a difference between getting inspired personally (yes we do need to do that, we need to take care of ourselves, but there is more).

There comes a point in life when we are not only interested in being inspired personally, but we start reaching out and inspiring other people, either through examples, through programs we run or the job that we have, or the goals that we have, and your life becomes more than just about you as an individual.

Being the inspiration- is the way that we lift up the people around us. It is the way that we get our message across and it is the way that we grow. Maybe you have a business or you are working in a company or you want to start something new, or maybe you lead a non-profit. It becomes important for you to have strategies and ways of being in place to be effective at and that is what I am going to share with you in this book, *Be the Inspiration: 7 Ways to Inspire Your World.*

By reading this book- you will be able to get tools and techniques that you can use right away. Upon reading this book, you might decide that you want to continue this conversation with me and I am going to tell you how you can do that and I am also going to offer you something special, too.

As we get started... I would love for you to set an intention for this book. I am a big fan of setting an intention for every experience in my life and I like to have my clients do it, too. So if you could hold for yourself, a space for your intention for reading this book - that would be fantastic.

Hold your hand over your heart... and ask:

What is my intention?

What specific piece do I want to learn?

Do I want to be inspired? Motivated?

Whatever it is for you personally- Set your intention. In my book, *Living Successfully and Joyfully Every Day: 90 Days of Inspiration* I talk about the importance of consciousness...and when we set an intention we are making a conscious choice.

For example, your intention might be getting motivated to act, and/or it might be getting clarity on a goal.

Some people who have heard and/or read the concepts included in this book experienced clarity around the program that they wanted to start or their next steps to take in their lives.

So go ahead and set an intention for yourself.

I want you to know that you do have the power and ability to overcome obstacles and not only achieve your dreams, but live successfully and joyfully every day.

Let's dive in, let's talk about the acronym INSPIRE.

The acronym INSPIRE:

I- I-story. Creating your compelling I-story.

N- New Beliefs,

S- Stepping into Inspired Action,

P- The Three P's: People, Purpose and Prosperity.

I-The second I is I love- it is all about unconditional love,

R- Reaching Out - which is your impact that you make on the world and also your ability to receive from the world.

E- Energy and Enthusiasm, where you successfully manage your energy and enthusiasm, and not just your own energy but the energy of your team, your company- whatever it is that is in your world.

Sometimes I have people ask me, "well I run my own company and I am really a solopreneur and I do not have a team, so how can I use this?"

Even as a solopreneur, you work with clients, vendors, joint venture partners, etc. For example, I was working with a vendor, and I started feeling that it was not working out and it was not aligning with my purpose of my business. I had to step back. That was part of managing the energy of my company and managing the energy of my business. Managing my own energy involved not letting that situation continue. Even if you are a solopreneur you will find the INSPIRE acronym applicable to your situation.

Let's begin our adventure together. Throughout this book I have included personal stories from colleagues and clients to help demonstrate the principles. I feel so blessed and honored to have these unique individuals bring you refreshingly honest and uplifting real stories. For even more resources, visit my website www.sherikayehoff.com

CHAPTER 2: I-*YOUR I-STORY*

Be that self which one truly is" **Soren Kierkegaard**

The first piece of Being the Inspiration involves your I-story.

Your I-story is all about you; it is all about your authentic you.

It's important to know and be who you really are. If I say to someone, "Tell me about you", that is the question that gets just about everyone flustered. It is because we sometimes have a hard time looking at ourselves or have a hard time knowing what the authentic self is really or what our message really is because we have layers and levels of ourselves.

There are different roles that we play in our lives and different things that we think we should do, but it is important to find the authentic you because that is how others resonate with you in the most powerful way.

It is your story that makes you unique. People like YOU. They do not want a version of you that is a copy of someone else, and it is vitally important to your leadership skills to be that authentic person. It is important if you own your own business. It is important, if you are a co-worker- if you are a colleague.

Be your authentic self because people intuitively know when you are being the authentic you and when you are not.

In my own story I talk about when I was a teenager, my younger brother took his own life. I came home from school when I was 17 years old and I found my 15 year old brother after he had killed himself, and it was a terrible, tragic shock. Prior to this devastating event, we had kind of a story book family. He was not in trouble or even depressed for a prolonged period. It was a total shock. This had a tremendous impact on our community and my family. I floundered for about seven years before I started to effectively put the pieces of my life back together.

This event in my life is part of my I-story and when I became comfortable with sharing that part of my life, my coaching practice grew. People want to know about your pain and struggles. They want to know that you triumphed. They want to know who you really are.

Now that doesn't mean that you have to have a terrible, tragic story in order to be interesting or in order to have compelling I-story. Your story could be one triumph after another and no little dips in your life, but guess what? That kind of story is inspiring, too. Everybody would want to know how you did it.

When I was comfortable sharing and reaching out to people with my story, my coaching practice really took off. Prior to that it was not that I was ashamed of my story in any way, but I had developed this professional persona in the corporate world and then in higher education where nobody knew that tragedy had happened and I did not want to be- *the girl whose brother died.* I did not want that to be my professional signature.

What I found is that sharing that part of me was sharing the real me.

People love stories, but they love the story even more if you can pull out some lessons learned. So with your compelling I-story you want to be able to come up with some key points that you can pull out of your story so that others can apply them to their lives.

One example of a lesson from my story is that as a result of my tragedy I had this view of myself that I could never be happy again. I thought, I might get to *okay* but I would never be really happy - like *skipping down the road* kind of happy.

However, I discovered happiness in my life through education, through working with the masters, through working on myself and through different programs. I realized the power of thought. I realized that I could choose the way that I felt. If I wanted to be happy I could choose happiness. That is an example of how I was in one place with my thoughts-thinking I am never going to be happy again and I found my way back to happiness and a happy lifestyle through my thoughts...

The lesson is that people have choice over the thoughts that they think.

With your authentic and compelling I-story, you want to be able to pull out and teach the lessons you learned so other people can benefit and use your experiences.

You might wonder where you will use your compelling I-story? You might use it on your website, you might use it on your blog, and you might use it in an introduction when people are introducing you on radio shows or at live events. You might use this story at networking events. Though I have to say when I am introducing myself to a complete stranger, I do not just blurt out my tragedy to triumph story abruptly; the story evolves through conversation.

However, when I am delivering a key note I do share the story.

Think about your own I-story right now because I want you to be able to apply this immediately. Think about your story.

What makes you unique? Think about one lesson that you could teach someone based on your life. For right now, think about one lesson and you do not have to write it all out in a paragraph, just write three to five word phrases, and if you want to expand on that great! Later, you can develop more lessons.

You will want to start merging your story into a tool that is motivating and inspiring to other people.

A big part of your compelling I-story is sharing mistakes. When I look back at my life, there were plenty of mistakes I made during that seven year span when I was floundering. I share some of those mistakes with my coaching clients. I share them and of course I made mistakes even after that, my goodness, it has been over 25 years.

But the point is: when you are willing to share your mistakes, you have that human connection plus the opportunity for learning is so powerful.

When I work with my clients who are coaches, I tell them about my first year trying to get my coaching business online and what a disaster it was because I did not know anything about online marketing. There are multiple blessings for others in the mistakes that I share. When my clients learn about my business mistakes in that first year, they save a lot of time and a lot of money. I feel passionate about helping other people from making those same mistakes that I made in the beginning.

Maybe you are not sure how to develop a compelling I-story. You might be thinking my job is: I am manager in a law firm or I am a manager of accountants or I own this business, for example.

You know what you are doing in terms of your career, but when it comes to being your authentic you, you might be thinking, "oh okay who is that really?" Maybe you have been trying to be someone different to please others.

Start with these prompts:

I love...

I am passionate about...

One day I had a question from a client- "how will I know when I am passionate?" and I knew what she was passionate about just by listening to her talk. When it seemed like she was "neutral" about a topic her voice was at a certain level, but when she started to get excited, then her voice started ramping up in volume and enthusiasm. Her enthusiastic voice involved her passions. This is one good reason to have a coach because I could hear her passion in her voice even though at the time, she couldn't hear it herself. It took an observation on my part.

You can notice passion within yourself by getting quiet with soft music and candles, and turning your mental and spiritual focus inward to your inner voice. Ask your intuition to reveal your passions. Be sure to keep a journal handy.

You can ask other people:

What do you love about me?

You can ask close friends, or close colleagues or a mentor,

What do you see in me?

Now be careful because if you ask your mom or dad they might be a little too close, because they knew you when you maybe got stuck up in a tree, when you tried to climb a tree and then could not get down. Obviously parents see us in a different light.

Ask yourself:

What do others love about me?

Where do I get complemented?

What just seems to flow naturally?

What can I teach blind folded?

Answering these questions gives you clues to your authentic self. I want to point out, additionally, that this process involves trial and error. There is no such thing as a perfect definition of your authentic self. Your authentic self evolves as you grow and change.

You will likely have times when you share your story and you find that you add pieces of your story or take pieces away.

Remember: there is no compelling I-story police walking around saying, "okay you got it right, or you got it wrong!"

Try a few different versions. I had another client share with me that, she has noticed that every time she shares her I-story – it changes and has grown quite a bit from the point in her life when she first started sharing it. Do not get nervous when your story changes a little bit; see this as a sign of growth.

Through practicing telling your story, you will start to get comfortable. I encourage you to tell your I-story and record it. Record it through audio acrobat or a conference line, or any method that you have of recording. Talk through it and then listen to how you sound. Remember: we do not have to be perfect to help other people.

*****

Here is an example of a compelling I-story from one of my colleagues.

Personal Story:

My Life Has Been Transformed Through Faith

By Pat Hastings

When I said "Yes" to God and let go of my fears, my life changed. I began to trust myself and the divine plan for my life. I stepped into my God power and am now doing what I love as an Author, Inspirational Speaker, Spiritual Coach & Radio Talk Show Host. I wrote a book called Simply a Woman of Faith: How to transform Your Life and Live in Spiritual Power. Today, I inspire audiences with my faith stories and everyday miracles about how I triumphed over family alcoholism, sexual abuse, the loss of a business, and healed from a traumatic divorce after 30 years of marriage. My passion is to help people connect with the God Power within, deepen their faith and find the divine purpose for their lives. Each day I open myself up to new possibilities and allow miracles to find me.

It was not always like that though. I thought I had to control everyone and everything around me. I tried to make things happen, rather than allow things to happen. It took me 7 years to write my book because I did not believe in myself and was filled with fear. I looked good on the outside, but inside I hated myself, did not feel good enough or deserving. I looked outside for my answers and became a people pleaser. I needed to ask a Power greater than myself to heal and change me.

Stepping into my God power meant that I had to change the negative messages that plagued me all of my life. I had a choice to either live in faith or fear. I chose faith. Plugging into the God Power within on a daily basis through prayer and meditation helped me take responsibility for myself and heal. When I do not plug in, it's easy to forget who I am as a child of God and the abundance that is rightfully mine.

In October 2008, I took a leap in faith and left my secure "good paying job" to start my own business doing what I love to do. My son said to me after I gave my notice, "Mom, this is the worst time for you to leave your job with this economy." Smiling, I said, "I know, but that's what God wants me to do." Through prayer and a series of synchronistic events, it became clear this was God's plan for my life.

Shortly after I gave my notice, I had what I call a "fear attack" and all the "what ifs", doubts and insecurities came rushing into my consciousness. Fear gripped me in the pit of my stomach and almost paralyzed me.

Through the grace of God, I was able to face my fear and move through it. Now I teach and inspire others how to transform their fears through faith.

I am grateful for the many doors and opportunities that have opened up since I left my job and started my business. I've been on TV and have had many radio interviews. Last year, I led a women's retreat in Bermuda, a women's workshop on a cruise ship and recently traveled to Hawaii to do a radio show. My weekly radio show is called "Finding the God of Your Understanding." My story and powerful message of faith makes me a sought after inspirational speaker, media guest, and workshop leader engaging audiences worldwide.

Saying "Yes" to God's divine plan takes courage and faith. I am grateful each day for the gift of life and the opportunities and miracles that are finding me.

Pat Hastings, Author of *Simply a Woman of Faith*

http://www.simplyawomanoffaith.com/

*****

Great elements in Pat's story include the fact that she shares mistakes, growth, lessons learned, and triumph. Her story is inspiring.

*****

Here is an example of a compelling I-story from one of my clients.

Personal Story:

The Adventurer

By Erin Ruiz

I have always considered myself an adventurer, always on a journey but it was recently that I had been on a different kind of voyage. Not your typical jump on a plane and head to the Bahamas kind of journey. This would be quite complex and out of the ordinary. This would be a quest to find my authentic self. I knew it would take honesty, humility, patience and acceptance to name a few for such a mission. Thirty odd years old and a single mom of two, I felt lost and the need more than ever to find happiness, inspiration and a voice. I spent years in pain and struggled for happiness and clarity. Would I be ready to delve into my soul to uncover my core beliefs and values? Would this journey help me seek out my hidden joys, talents and confidence? Unfortunately, my journey was put on hold due to an illness or was it?

Let me take you back a few years when I suffered from debilitating migraines. My vision was blurred, I had palpitations, and a never ending pounding heartbeat in my ear. I had a hard time swallowing, especially at night, when I would awake choking. Sometimes my arm or leg would go numb. My specialist continued to treat me for migraines and give me a prescription that would supposedly help the migraine, except it did not. Years passed and I still continued to have the horrid pain. I would frequent the emergency room many times a month. Nothing new uncovered. I was beyond frustrated! Where was my voice?

I knew I needed an MRI, and with a lot of persuasion I was under the scope. I went to the neurologist to have them read it. It was in that cold, uninviting office that my neurologist read me my results that would change my life forever. She proceeded to tell me that I had a brain abnormality called Chiari Malformation and that it was no big deal. A million and one things ran through my head. She wanted to continue treating me for migraines. We need not worry about the chiari.

At that very moment, I fired that neurologist and walked out. I was overwhelmed! Did this really just happen? No big deal? It was the turning point in my life where I finally acknowledged my voice! My confidence rose, I questioned my values and beliefs and started to lead by example. I became passionate about research and education. I sought after the best of the best neurosurgeons. I refused for anything less.

Fast forward a few years and twenty or so specialists later, I learned a lot about the brain and the spinal cord and the way it functions and how our life depends on these vital parts to give and receive information. I learned that a chiari malformation is when your brainstem is herniated into your foramen magnum. Basically that means that there is too much brain to contain and not a lot of space for your cerebral spinal fluid to pass properly. It can cause a barrage of symptoms and utter internal chaos, sometimes leads to paralysis.

In those exhaustive years, I endured a ten hour spinal cord surgery, brain surgery and survived a pulmonary embolism. My determination and strength helped unveil beautiful authentic me. I became an advocate to help raise awareness with walks, talking to everybody and even teaching my Doc a thing or two. Chiari has no cure yet, but with research, awareness and patience, we are one step closer! Life is forever with ups and downs, but the good news is, when you are down the only way is up! What a blessing this part of my journey has been!

Erin Ruiz

*****

Erin's story is so authentic and compelling. She shares heartbreak, perseverance, setbacks, and yet she still has an overall, positive upbeat attitude.

You have just experienced two amazing stories from two fabulous women. My hope is that you are on your way to writing your authentic I-story.

Many have found platforms for businesses and new ideas for products through developing their I-stories. No one else is you or has your perspective, so when you approach your work life, your biz, and your personal life from the strength of authenticity, you have truly struck gold.

"Fortune befriends the bold."
Emily Dickinson

"Begin, be bold and venture to be wise.' Horace

CHAPTER 3: N- NEW BELIEFS

"Every human has four endowments- self awareness, conscience, independent will and creative imagination. These give us the ultimate human freedom... The power to choose, to respond, to change." Stephen Covey

Next- let's move into discussing new beliefs.

Stephen Covey's book, 7 *Habits of Highly Effective People* is one of my early inspirations in the 90's and probably one of the reasons why I am a life coach today. I read it at a difficult time in my life. I was on bed rest as a 25 year old and I could only get up three minutes every hour for 11 weeks. It sounded like a jail sentence to me and so learning that my mind was free no matter what was going on with my body was a really cool thing for a

25 year old and it spurred my interest in leadership, self development, and self-help that served me well throughout my career and developing a business.

I view beliefs as the operating system of your life. What you believe is your truth and your reality. Whatever you believe shapes your abilities, capabilities, capacity to succeed, and ultimately, what you achieve in your life. If you are not achieving what you want, the place to look first is your belief system.

"You can have anything you want if you will give up the belief that you can't have it." Dr Robert Anthony

I love this quote. Our beliefs drive our success or our lack of success. What do you want? Start seeing it and believing it. Stop saying to yourself- "It will never happen" – and stop looking for excuses or someone or something to blame. Believe... I believe in you. I know that if you can believe in you- you will see that goal happen. I have witnessed many talented individuals, teams, organizations- who never really believe and they plateau or slide backwards...

If you struggle with belief... use affirmations to help you turn this around. Simple statements like- I believe in my skills. I believe that I deserve to perform at a high level. I believe that I am worthy. I believe that I can do it. I believe … (create your own personal statement).

Practice these statements and also notice your own self- talk – be aware- notice when you say… "I can't do it"…

With some diligence, you will find yourself shifting to a stronger, winning set of beliefs.

Also consider this, are you thinking small? Do you think in terms of the minimum you need to sustain your work, your personal finances, or any other goal? When you think small… you consistently bring in those results that correspond to your small thoughts. What would happen if you thought big? Take one area of your life… and expand your thinking… think big. For example, instead of thinking… I just want to pay my bills… Think… what do I need to do to not only pay my bills and have a cushion of X amount of money every month? Whenever you set a goal, add some cushion to it. Here is another example of thinking bigger- when you think of your dream home… imagine not just the dream home, but the furnishings inside, the money to comfortably maintain the home, pay the taxes, join the country club, plus a cushion. Are you getting the idea?

You can apply this thinking big idea to everyday situations, too. For instance, a common thought might be... I need to find the time to exercise. Change this to I want the time to exercise, sit in the hot tub/sauna/steam room, showering, etc – don't think in minimums- think about everything you truly want to happen, plus a cushion.

Thinking big gives you big results. *Believe in Thinking Big.*

Exercise: Ask yourself- where I am thinking too small in my life? How can I add big thinking to this area? When you shift to thinking big in this area, track your results. Keep reminders in clear sight about your commitment to thinking big.

Challenge your beliefs about yourself and think big.

When we talk about beliefs in relationship to leadership, there are some beliefs that are in the way, others that are inspiring to other people and empowering. The good news about belief systems is that you can adopt new beliefs, you have choice. So if you have beliefs that are not supportive of you and your goals, you can exchange those or change them completely.

Let's look at some top beliefs that get in the way of success.

The belief that other's success takes away from your success which creates a feeling of competition, a feeling of jealousy. This belief gets in the way of a mentoring relationship or a leadership position. When you have someone that you are mentoring, become successful- do you feel great about it, or do you think I wish that was my success?

Other negative beliefs include:

- The need for micro-management,
- People are untrustworthy,
- People are demanding,
- There is never enough time.
- The need to rush all the time.

Did you see yourself in any of those negative beliefs?

Did you notice additional negative beliefs that are not listed?

That is okay because, again your beliefs involve choice. You can choose differently.

Let's look at some new beliefs, and these are beliefs of a leader. They are beliefs of one who inspires other people and remember- you can lead from any position.

Everyone can learn and possess great leadership skills no matter what official position they hold. Leadership has to start somewhere, a few people experience an official leadership title, and then, there are people who naturally lead from where they are. So make a commitment to integrate excellent personal leadership skills into your life starting right now.

Here are some positive beliefs of a leader.

- I have a message.
- I make a difference.
- I care about others,
- I lift up others.
- I create synergy,
- I believe in myself.
- I believe I can do it.
- I also believe we can do it.
- I believe in honoring what I need.
- I believe my time is valuable, yet I have plenty of time to accomplish the importance things.
- I manage my energy,
- I live a life of consciousness,
- I believe in other's ability to contribute.
- I believe people are good hearted.

So you can see some of the positive beliefs are about what you believe about yourself, and some are about your beliefs about other's abilities.

Of course your beliefs about yourself create who you are....and what you believe about other people tends to come true, as well. I am not saying leave your car unlocked or do not lock your house or do not have a security system. However, in general, in your work and personal roles- hold the belief that people are good hearted.

I believe that people are good hearted and apply this in almost every single situation. I believe this whether he or she is a prospective coaching client, a vendor, a front line person, a customer service representative, etc. Across just about every single experience that I have- I see that people are great. I experience positive outcomes and nice people.

I have determined the reason why I have these terrific people experiences is that I have a basic belief that people are good hearted. People sense this and have a tendency to live up to it.

Though you can change and choose your beliefs, this takes diligence and determination. Beliefs tend to be persistent. So do not give up if you find the path a bit difficult. Affirmations, prayer, and meditation help. Reading inspiring stories of triumph over negative experiences helps. Coaching and journaling also will boost your ability to implement and integrate more positive beliefs.

You also want to be aware of the beliefs of your team at work, your family at home, your friends, etc. You really can positively impact the creation of more empowering team beliefs.

A great example of this involves my son's football coach. When my son was on the ten year old tackle football team, they won their first game, then, the second game, they were beaten badly. After the game, the coach was encouraging- he talked about the things the team performed well and then confidently discussed the things they could improve. All the boys were happy. They were happy that they could see a solution and left still believing in themselves. In the same situation, the coach could have destroyed their confidence and made them fearful for the next game. This is the true test of leadership. Can you keep your team believing and performing through the difficult times? This is truly what I mean when I say- Be the Inspiration.

Exercise: Write a short article or blog post on the impact of beliefs on one's personal life and/or career. If you do not have a blog yet go to wordpress.com and you can create one and have it up and running in five minutes. Developing a blog can be one of the most effective ways to establish an online reputation and credibility in your field.

CHAPTER 4: STEP INTO INSPIRED ACTION

"Do what you can, with what you have, wherever you are."~ Theodore Roosevelt

Our next leg of our journey together is stepping into inspired action and this also involves inspiring by example. In your own world, in your own environment, you want to be taking inspired action. I remember years ago when I worked in the corporate world, I was willing to do what needed to be done whether it was a small or large task.

I had no problem taking my trash out of my office when it was full and even taking it out to the dumpster. The point is that I did not look at the trash and think· "oh my trash is full, when is somebody going to come and empty it?" I jumped up and took care of it. Did

I do that all the time, no! But I did not look at any task as beneath me...

I also created project proposals and change management plans that were a few levels above my responsibility and they sometimes ended up on the president's desk and were then implemented. I could have thought- I see a need, but that is not my responsibility- instead I saw a need and shared an idea. You can lead from any position.

Be the person who steps into inspired action and make sure that you have created room for success and room for failure. People won't act if there is fear. Create an empowering company culture. Some of you can probably relate to the fact that you may have worked or are still working for a company with a company culture based on fear. It is hard to get people to act if they are afraid to make any mistakes.

Create room for both success and failure and think about how you react when there is a failure. Do you ask, "Can I get this to work?" Or do you have a *sky is falling* kind of mentality? Do you often think or say- "oh this is terrible" and list all the reasons why it is so awful that this mistake or failure happened.

I am not saying failure is great, but if you want to really tap creativity and inspired action you want to make sure that people know that it is ok to make a mistake here and there.

Inspired action is closely tied to intrinsic motivation. Look at your own intrinsic motivation. Your intrinsic motivation is motivation from within and I would say it is not the carrot, it is not the stick. It is not motivation for reward and it is not motivation from evading punishment, it is motivation that comes from within.

You know you have this when you are psyched up to do something. When you are working on a project and you feel like you could work indefinitely without looking up. For example, often I am writing and I get lost for 6 hours or more and I feel like only 20 minutes have passed by because I am so engrossed and absorbed. I become so inspired by what I am doing. This is a different scenario than when you have a deadline around something that you are dreading or something you definitely do not like to do. Time creeps by and it becomes difficult to stay focused.

Yes, there are going to be things that are not your favorite thing to do, so I suggest that you find some way to make it fun. My colleague, Jeanna Gabellini, was talking to me once and she said that she puts on loud rock music and makes it crazy fun when she has to do her taxes because that is her thing. She does have an accountant but she still has to gather everything together. She has found a way to get the motivation to be able to do it through making it fun.

There could be another level of motivation through creating a deeper appreciation for your finances in your life and that can push you to move forward and act, too.

If you own property take care of it. A burned out light bulb sends a message of lack and not replacing a light bulb sends a message that you cannot care for what you already own. This puts an entirely different perspective in getting those light bulbs changed. Think of a building maintenance person in charge of changing those light bulbs and when he or she looks at the job as just changing light bulbs it is a completely different view than looking at it as- "my job impacts the overall message of this company, my job is part of how people feel when they walk in the door and how safe they feel and how cared for they feel." So you see how motivation will be more intrinsic when it is based on pride of the individuals involved.

Being motivated by external rewards and punishment does not compare to the joy of finding intrinsic motivation.

You not only want to find intrinsic motivation for yourself but you want to help other people tap into it as well.

You may have experienced a job, where there might be a big reward, a bonus that the company offers, and no one' s sales increased as a result of it. Everybody pretty much stayed the same. The reward was not (in people's eyes), motivating. So you can throw money at a situation to try to make it better and have it not work at all.

How can you cultivate intrinsic motivation? You need a cohesive message and purpose that others can rally behind. People need to understand- why they are doing something. Even in the family, people need to understand- okay I am helping straighten up the house to get ready for this party and this party is important because (whatever the reason is). People pitch in because they understand the why.

I remember one time my husband called me saying (we had a car for sale), "someone is on the way to make an offer on the car, I won't make it there I am still at work, they want to look at the car".

It was a car that I happened to be driving regularly, and I said to my kids, "someone is going to be here in 20 minutes and dad always says clean sells" and so we just jumped into the car, started cleaning it- vacuuming. It was not terribly dirty but we made it sparkle and the person bought it on the spot. The help I received from my kids came from their understanding of why we were doing it. I did not even have to ask them. I just described the situation and they headed for the vacuum. We headed for the car and they knew what to do because they understood why they were doing it.

We can take this example of a cohesive message to an organizational level. In my company when I am working with virtual assistants or working with other people who are working on my team they understand how their piece fits in the whole big picture of my business. There is dynamic action.

When a person knows that his or her piece makes the difference, and understands what difference it makes, he or she is motivated to do- to act. A cohesive message is a vital aspect of stepping into inspired action.

Inspired action is also a result of effective planning.

I know you have thoughts about what you want to accomplish, but do those thoughts make it on paper or in a spreadsheet? When you devote time to creating a plan for not just your biz or professional life, but also your personal life, you achieve more.

Does planning seem overwhelming? It doesn't have to be. Even a simple, one page plan is effective. As you think about your plan, notice themes that pop out.

Maybe this is a year of travel for you, a year of spiritual growth, a year of rapid financial recovery and growth, a year of learning, etc... Once you get a clear idea of what you want to do, you can then break it down into manageable pieces. Remember this is your plan, so you have the power to change it. There are no *plan police* out there to write you a ticket for creating an incorrect plan. So what are you waiting for? Get that plan in place...

"The best way to predict the future is to invent it." – Immanuel Kant

This quote is so empowering. Wondering what the future holds? Your effort at planning is your part of inventing it. So, what in the world do you want to do? Start with a brainstorming list... write down at least 25 things that you want to do ... do this freestyle and free flow... meaning do not judge what you write down as it comes to your mind... Include things from all parts of your life. Make it fun, turn on uplifting music, draw pictures – you could even use big paper and makers. If you have kids, have them do it, too. This is a great beginning to creating a plan.

Yes, plans are great, we have to have plans but if you have all the plans in the world and no action behind them ˙nothing happens. You probably know someone who is all plans and no action. You have to do – you have to act. Jump in˙ get things in motion. Move forward. At some point, you will have to take the plunge.

Being inspired, being led from spirit, being led from your intuition (your inner self) is a dynamic way to be and act.

Developing your intuition for better decision making is a transforming way to approach life. We sometimes find that we are on the fence or maybe even completely confused regarding the next step, but our inner compass always knows the way... the right next step. When I say "intuition" I mean divine guidance and/or guidance from your higher or inner self.

One of my favorite techniques for developing intuition is asking a question before I fall asleep. I might say something like, "I would like clarity on my next step for my business, and when I wake up, I want to know my next move. Above all, I want to feel the rightness of it." Then, while I am sleeping my subconscious and my inner, higher self are working on the idea. Many times, I wake up with a certainty about what to do next.

Another method to help you develop your intuition is to get quiet and set the intention, "I am looking for the answer to... (insert topic) and when an answer comes to me, I will know beyond a shadow of a doubt that it is my intuition that is guiding me."

I am not dismissing logic or research, as these are important steps, but intuition allows us to make leaps instead of maybe mere baby steps forward. I use a combination of processes in decision making, but have found intuition to be the most reliable.

When you are making decisions about taking inspired action, intuition is a valuable asset.

If you are having a hard time with clarity around your decision making or planning, do a heart check. Your heart knows what it wants. Get quiet, put your hand over your heart... ask, "What is my heart telling me?"

You may find the answer pops up immediately or you may find that you just get an overall, peaceful feeling... knowing the answer is on its way to revealing itself. You might also feel nothing... that is okay.

It takes practice to settle yourself down in order to be able to listen to your heart. However, the reward is great. You find yourself living a life of purpose and passion instead of a life of *shoulds* and *have tos*.

See clearly with your heart, today...

Respecting other people's inner value systems is also important to enabling inspired action. Ultimately you want to create a high trust environment. And the best way to do this is that you do what you say you will do and be consistent. When you keep your word and you are consistent it sends a powerful message to people around you. Probably everyone has an example of working in a low trust environment at some point, and hopefully you have had some examples of working in a high trust environment. High trust environments are highly productive. Stephen M. R. Covey wrote the book, *The Speed of Trust* which is a great book about how important trust is within our organizations. In fact, much business today is still conducted on the basis of a handshake.

A high trust environment allows for more inspired action.

When you combine your own role model example of you taking inspired action and then add in an empowering environment, intrinsic motivation, effective planning, and high trust- you will see people around you taking their own inspired action steps.

*****

Personal Story

Africa

By Nancy Falconi

Ask the animals, and they will teach you, or the birds of the air, and they will tell you; or speak to the earth, and it will teach you, or let the fish of the sea inform you."

--Job 12:7-8

Several years ago I left a well established career as a Business Professor & Human Resource Manager to pursue my passion for photography. It has slowly step by step; led to experiences I would have never dreamed of, one of those was traveling to Tanzania, Africa.

Little did I know it all started one day when a friend invited me to the reception for the opening of her new art gallery. At the art gallery there was a large photograph of a zebra that really caught my eye. Looking at the image, I said to myself "I could do that, mmm, no I would L O V E to do that... if only I could go to Africa ..." The thought had never even crossed my mind before that night, as I had pursued my photography career on a more commercial basis; because I thought that was the best way to make a living from photography. I started the mental chatter in my head, "I can't just go to Africa, and I will go when my kids are older, when my business is more stable..."

At this point my commercial photography business was not faring well financially. I made substantial investments moving to digital photography just as the traditional use of print photography was on the decline, and the economic downturn only made matters worse. My accountant told me to consider bankrupting my business.

Shifting to a creative entrepreneur has been a crash course exploration of Self for me; illuminating my innate talents and gifts and also my deepest fears. It has taught me to rely on my own instincts and to trust them to lead me in the right direction.

Despite what my rational mind told me, I got a loan to fund my business and started to take a number of courses in drawing, painting, film & storytelling. I decided to take my career in the direction of what I loved (as opposed to what I thought my customers wanted).

There comes a point when pursuing your passion, is all you can think about even when at present it does not make any sense.

Traveling to Africa was one of those instinct led actions. I had this inner knowing that guided me to this trip. In Africa experiencing animals in their natural environment first-hand impressed upon me very strongly how they are solely guided by their instincts, how they rely and trust them unequivocally, and how reliable they are. It has strengthened my resolve to follow my own inner guidance in my life. The trip was definitely a highlight of my life, everything about the trip unfolded perfectly.

While in Africa, one night as I was getting ready to go to sleep I heard this strange sound outside the window of my lodge. I opened the curtains and staring right back at me about 4 feet away was a zebra. I was in a state of complete shock. I don't think it was a coincidence that it was a zebra in the art gallery who led me to Africa in the first place. I knew that encounter had great meaning for me.

The zebra signaled clarity (black and white) and trust for me in my life. The symbolism of the zebra has been an anchor, as I go through some major shifts in my life:

Zebra: "When zebra comes into your life, change is signified in one or more areas of your life and hidden knowledge will be uncovered. Stand strong; develop trust and simply flow with the rhythm of a new creation."

www.shamanicjourney.com

Animals and signs from nature have been very important guides for me, leading me to a more authentic life, not just in Africa in my own backyard as well. I believe animals can help us reclaim parts of us we have lost and help guide us towards our dreams.

So far the trip to Africa has opened up some of my most cherished accomplishments; I have created a book on elephants - called "Elephants Up Close." The purpose of the book is to illustrate the importance of developing an awareness and dialogue with nature and animals -with information and images of elephants as an example.

Also, I have just been accepted to a juried art show based on the images in the book in which I am creating encaustic paintings and photographs, another dream. Maybe next, I'll work on zebras, and who knows what is next...

Nancy Falconi, Artist, Photographer

www.nancyfalconi.com

*****

Nancy took inspired action and it led to the experience of her dreams.

*****

Exercise: Use the action plan steps below.

Action Plan Steps

- State Your Goal.
- Information gathering: research, intuition, and experience.
- Create steps and identify milestones.
- List needed resources.
- Create a timeline.
- Act on steps.
- Celebrate milestones.
- Evaluation Plan (weekly? 30 days? 90 days? Etc) Decide what constitutes success...Decide what's next...

CHAPTER 5: P- 3 P'S PEOPLE, PURPOSE, AND PROSPERITY

3 P's – People

Do all the good you can, by all the means you can, in all the ways you can, in all the places you can, at all the times you can, to all the people you can, as long as ever you can.- **John Wesley's Rule**

Our next part of our Be the Inspiration journey together is exploring the three P's: people, purpose, and prosperity.

Always remember that people are your number one resource and to get anything done in your life you need people.

Therefore, you need to act actively assess who you need in your life. You want to see who is around you right now, notice who is in your life already- your business partners, your colleagues, your family, your neighbors, your clients, etc.

Then, consider who you need to find and attract into your life and who do you need to let go. There might be a few. The better you get at attracting the right people, the less people you need to let go.

Determine to find the wisdom, support, and skills that you need. Let's say you have a guru or someone who is the best in your field and you want to get access their information. Attend a class that they are offering or get their book. Learn from other people. Set the intention that the right people will come into your life. Sometimes attracting the right people comes about in a surprising way.

Here is the story about how I ended up interviewing Marci Shimoff on my Your Path to Success Telesummit series. I saw her in the movie the Secret and I liked her message, and I liked her energy. I thought, I would love to collaborate with her someday in something but I never really put much thought into it other than putting that intention out there to the universe and reading her books.

I was not thinking about how I was going to work with her but it just so happened that I ended up interviewing Michael Linenberger.

He is the author of *Master your Work Day Now* and he was dating Marci at the time (I had no idea when I booked him). I then, ended up interviewing Marci the next year when her book, Love for No Reason launched. What I did was set the intention and then be open to possibilities.

It is really wonderful how things work out. Do not worry about how you are going to get the right people but concentrate on the kinds of people that you want in your circle of influence, and what their role might be. Set about determining who the right people are.

One of my favorite affirmations is: "I am so happy and so thankful that the right people are coming into my life at exactly the right time"- and most of the time it happens.

Another aspect of tapping people's expertise is asking, "What would Oprah do in this situation? What would (insert your favorite expert) do in this situation?" Etc. If you have read their work and studied them, chances are you will have a good idea about how they might handle a situation. It's like having a whole panel of experts at your fingertips.

*****

Personal Story

By Crystal Lynn Miller

Listening to Divine guidance and following my intuition has been an important aspect in the unfolding of my life. A good example of this happened when I became extremely unhappy in a relationship that I felt very committed to.

Personally, I was in a time of great spiritual awareness and expansion before things started to go seriously wrong in the relationship. I was meditating, participating in Healing Touch International classes, had learned how to move energy in my body, and my intuitive abilities were really opening up. All this just added to the very spiritual and prayerful life I had already been living. It was amazing! I experienced God and my angels speaking to me through dreams, songs, books that I would just happen to pick up, or that "knowing" I would feel during prayer and meditation. Sometimes I was guided to say or do something "out of the blue" that would have a profound effect on the course of my life.

When things started to go "wrong" in the relationship, my angels gave me concrete information and guidance. I would have an intuitive knowing about things that were not shared with me honestly by my partner. I would have dreams at night that would show me the truth of what was going on, what was out of integrity in the relationship and what needed to be addressed.

This is not about blame. This is about Divine assistance in a relationship that did not have love at the center of it. This is guidance so that we could get out a dysfunctional pattern and on to our own paths. This guidance was a gift. For me, it was my angels saying, "You deserve more than this." I was resistant at first because I did not want to let go of the relationship for several reasons, but finally, I surrendered after constant messages from heaven. I chose to no longer run from the truth.

I set aside time to go outside and do a walking meditation and some centering energy techniques that assist in connection to the Divine. I prayed, "Dear God, I am now willing to see the truth of this situation. I am open to hearing Divine guidance about the steps that I need to take that are for my highest good." I became truthful with myself about my own needs. I desired to be in a more loving relationship, to do the work that I am here to do and to be the best possible "me" that I could.

This is what I heard, "Your purpose in life is to experience joy. When you experience joy and love, it naturally flows within and around you, and others will benefit. But first, the focus is on creating joy in your own life! It is important to know that you deserve to receive and experience good in all ways. You can stay in the relationship, but you will not experience joy and spiritual expansion at the depths that are available to you. The relationship dynamics and turmoil distracts you. The choice is yours, but if you were to let go of your attachment to this particular relationship working out, reach for the stars with your desires and let yourself receive the good that is yours, then you will experience so much greater joy, love and spiritual awareness."

"Yes, to greater love, joy and spiritual expansion!" was my answer.

I was able to let go and felt peaceful and reassured about this choice. I was excited about the new opportunities that I KNEW would unfold in my life. Partners do not always need to go in different directions, especially if they are both willing to heal the relationship, but given my situation, it was for *the highest good. Since then, I have experienced joy, love and spiritual awareness at greater depths just as I was told I would, and it just keeps getting better!*

I am so thankful for Divine guidance!

Crystal Lynn Miller, Energy Healing Practitioner

www.CrystalLynnMiller.com

*****

Crystal's story vividly demonstrates the importance of being willing to let go and honoring the highest good for herself and others.

*****

Exercise:

People Needs Assessment and Communication Assessment

Identify the People in Your Life:

- Your Inner Circle (people you deeply trust- would trust with your biggest secrets and your life):
- Your Middle Circle (people you trust to be honest, do what they say most of the time)

- Your Outer Circle (people you trust with some things...)
- People just outside your circle (people who are not in your circle of trust but are in your life in some way)
- Who do you need to move around?
- Who do you need to meet and add to your circle? Create a strategy for attracting the right people to you

Your Communication Assessment- rate yourself (create positive affirmations and strategies for low scoring areas):

- Courteous (1 to 10 highest)
- Compassionate (1 to 10)
- Caring (1 to 10)
- Ability to learn about what is most important to others (1 to 10)
- Helpful (1 to 10)
- Accepting (1 to 10)
- Not demanding (1 to 10)
- Listening (1 to 10)
- Ability to share your own needs (1 to 10)
- Ability to ask for help (1 to 10)
- Ability to give constructive feedback (1 to 10)
- Ability to build a high trust environment (1 to 10)
- Setting effective boundaries (1 to 10)

- On time for appointments/meetings (1 to 10)
- Keep commitments (1 to 10)
- Ability to meet new people with ease (1 to 10)

3 P's- Purpose

Part of the 3 P's is purpose, having a driving purpose behind everything that you do. It involves knowing why are you doing this? Why do you have a business? I think business should be fun and I have a mantra- if it is not fun, I do not want to do it. I love to have fun with what I am doing and my driving purpose is also more than fun. People usually have a driving purpose that is a higher purpose. For example, mentoring business people, mentoring young people, mentoring people who are ill are examples of purpose. Your purpose could be helping people make a change in their lives. Usually a higher purpose is something beyond; "I want to make a million dollars this year".

I think making a million dollars is fantastic, so I am not saying exclude that but include a purpose that is higher ordered and part of making a significant contribution.

For me purpose is all about people, for me it is about mentoring, it is about caring for people as individuals and caring for people in groups. I feel an energetic connection to everyone I work with. Once someone is in my circle, they are never out of it, even if I work with somebody for half an hour, that person becomes part of who I am. This connection is part of my driving purpose.

I am like this no matter what group I work with including my friends, my daughter's cheerleading team, a group of kids at church, kids in the neighborhood, I love, love working with people. So whatever I am doing I am giving 100% of myself in that capacity.

Live a life of purpose and passion- sounds ideal and simple, yet it is elusive many. How do you figure out your purpose? The difficulty lies in the fact that we have devoted much of our lives doing things because we *should* do them and we give little thought to whether we are really doing what we want to be doing.

Clues about your purpose in life abound... when you look back over your life, you can probably see common themes around things that you loved doing. You have talents and skills which often point to purpose. And your purpose can evolve over time. Your purpose might expand as you gain a bigger vision for life as you see more possibilities.

When I work with people who are truly living a life of purpose, there is usually a sense of alignment about their lives- things feel right. If you feel out of alignment, that is a sign that you need to make some changes and shifts.

Try things out. Try on new ideas and new directions. Use intuition to guide you by getting quiet and turning inward. Journaling helps this process.

When you live your purpose, life is exciting and fulfilling.

In determining your purpose...list out ten things you are passionate about...and then keep narrowing the list down... you might want to try Janet Attwood's book *The Passion Test* to help you.

Finding your purpose doesn't have to be hard...it can be flowing and easy- if you intend it to be that way. Finding your purpose is also a lifelong journey as you will notice changes as you grow.

*****

Personal Story:

The Ripple Effect of Purpose:

By Nancy Farris, Life Coach, Muse

Have you ever wondered why connection to purpose is so important? I'd like to share an experience from my own life.

At the end of last year, I was meeting with a client who has enrolled me as her "Blog Muse."

My role as her "muse" is twofold. First to make sure visitors to her blog experience her unique personality and "voice." Secondly, as her muse I partner with her as we create a path to make blog writing totally fun for her.

On this particular day, we met in a local coffee shop. As our conversation began, she handed me a post she'd written that described in great detail, a recent art experiment she had embraced.

As I read her draft, I was immediately struck by the complete absence of her playful personality. When asked how she felt about what she'd written, she admitted the post did not speak to her at all. Whew. Okay, it was not just me.

We immediately put her draft aside, and proceeded to discover what her spirit truly wanted her to say about her new art adventure. As the conversation evolved, we both became more and more animated.

I watched in awe as her whole being sprung to life. I was having a ton of fun, and it seemed to me that she was, too.

Then something totally unexpected happened. A stranger walked up to our table, introduced himself, apologized for the intrusion, and then complimented us on how well we worked together. He then added that he so enjoyed watching our interaction, he just had to stop and tell us.

Wow. I think that's the first time in my life that's ever happened.

As I later reflected on the 'meaning' of the encounter, it suddenly hit me. I had taken on part-time work in the past year, while growing my coaching business. While very grateful for the additional income, the work did not bring my soul the kind of joy that I feel when working (okay, playing!) with my clients.

Also, the role of Muse was a different slant from my usual coaching, and I was not quite sure how it would unfold. Knowing that the spirit of the interaction with my client rippled through the coffee shop – enough to move a stranger to comment, I knew there was an important message in it for me. And as I reflected on that message, I knew I had connected with my true purpose.

When I see someone whose being seems to be totally lit up, chances are they're connected with their purpose. It's very attractive, and often quite obvious. Yet, when we're connected to our purpose, the flow sometimes feels so easy and joyful, it can be easy to take it for granted and we might miss the connection. (That's why even we coaches have coaches!)

Years of trying to "figure out" my purpose did not get me much closer to discovering it. By creating opportunities to play with others in ways that truly bring me tremendous joy... I believe I created the space for my purpose to find me, and allowed it to be reflected back to me.

If you, too, have spent a lifetime wondering about or looking for your purpose, consider dropping the pursuit of it and create an intention to be present in each moment, live in joy, and cultivate awareness.

When you pay attention, I believe you will notice when your purpose finds you – and if by some chance you miss it, perhaps the Universe will reflect it back to you. In any event, chances are it will be quite obvious to those around you.

Living life through the lens of your purpose, not only impacts your life and the joy you experience, but the effect ripples through to everyone in your orbit.

We often do not realize the impact we have on people we do not personally meet.

Nancy Farris, Life Coach, Muse

www.yourmagicallife.com

*****

Nancy gives a very creative and inspirational view about discovering purpose. She is a very much needed catalyst or muse in this world.

*****

Personal Story

Trading Dollars for Hours Stopped

By Doug Jarvie, Life Coach

I am a life coach! I have spent 30 years getting educated, 30 years working for others, now I explore the opportunities for the next 60 years and embrace the changes.

The education has not stopped, and will not until I die. It includes certification as an Electronic Technician, a BSC in Honors Physics, Post grad diploma in E-commerce, ongoing education in manufacturing management and programming for embedded systems. Most recently I have earned certification in life coaching and spiritual coaching.

The working for others, trading hours for dollars, stopped when I came to the conclusion that my time was worth more to me than others were willing to pay for it. Now I work on my schedule and am at liberty to let the creative side live again.

I am changing! Now the changes are by choice, not forced upon me. Now I choose how I react to the changes in my environment, and choose to be the agent of change rather than the one who asks "what happened?" after it is all over.

I was born into a family of a father who had returned from Hong Kong the year before, where he had been a POW for 5 years, a brother almost 12 years older who lived with cerebral palsy and required constant assistance to dress, eat, walk and take care of personal hygiene, and a mother who held it all together.

Like many people I was given the spiritual gift of helping. I was placed into an environment where it was very easy for me to use that gift. I was 11 years old when my father died and I was able to use that gift even more fully.

I began working behind the scenes, with the machine, behind the screen. I learned that others could do some things better than I, and that by coordinating our efforts we could accomplish more, better, faster. I learned that communication with others became better and easier as I learned more about myself and others. That is where I am focusing by learning efforts.

Like a sponge, I have soaked up a lot of pieces of information, some of which are timeless principles which do not change; some which are transient procedures which are always changing.

Like a sponge, in order to give up this information, I need to be squeezed a little.

Doug Jarvie, Life Coach

www.dougjarvie.com

*****

Doug's story shows us how purpose evolves through a lifetime. We are always growing and shifting and developing more awareness regarding purpose.

Exercise: Create a statement of purpose for your life. This could be a paragraph or multiple pages.

3 P's – Prosperity

The next P is prosperity. You must have a prosperity mindset, if you do not have a prosperity mindset work on it. You might be thinking- I am not sure this mindset thing will work for me. And I will show you why it works. Say to yourself 3 times, "this is a disaster, this is a disaster and this is a disaster". Notice how you feel. Did you get a sinking feeling and sink into your chair? Did your head drop a bit?

And then say "I am strong, I am strong, I am strong". You definitely feel something different energetically. Did you straighten up, lift your head? How you talk to yourself, makes a difference and if it can make a difference even when you say a word that you are not really thinking about, just think about what happens when you are putting powerful thought behind those words and beliefs.

Your mindset is your most powerful ally or enemy in your life. You do have the ability to successfully manage your thought life. I encourage you to use this life-changing paradigm immediately.

The work you do in creating an empowering, goal achieving mindset, yields immediate results. You will rapidly move yourself towards your goals as you continuously affirm what it is that you want and remove your focus from what you do not want.

Make an effort to use positive language in your self-talk and your conversations with others. Turn everything into a focus on the desired outcome and not on what you want to avoid.

Every time you talk to yourself in a, "oh my goodness this bill is due, I do not know how I am going to meet that" or any sort self talk that comes from a place of lack, you can change it to: "wouldn't it be nice if it was really easy to pay this bill? Wouldn't it be nice if there really was more than enough?" So just asking yourself- *wouldn't it?...* will help lift you to a different, more prosperous mind set. And that is important for you as an individual and you as a leader. Your prosperity mindset affects the energy of your team.

Every moment of every day we have choice. We can choose a better feeling thought. Each subject has a positive side and a negative side. For instance, if you have a bill and you constantly tell yourself- "how am I going to make that payment?" And you stress about it every month- you are feeling the negative side of the experience.

On the other hand, if you have a bill every month and you tell yourself, "I got this." "It's easy-peasy" "I am paying for something I highly value and my payment is worthwhile." "I appreciate the services or product I receive in exchange for my payment". You are on the positive feeling side of the experience.

The negative feelings bring struggle- and you will have the experience of difficulty in your finances. The positive feelings bring solutions and an easier flow of money.

You probably recognize your own situations regarding positive and negative... Look at your results and trace them back to your thought processes. In fact, keep a journal and record your thoughts... you will begin to recognize patterns.

Start using more positive language and cultivate positive thoughts around your goals. Use language that demonstrates achievement, possibilities, happiness, joy. The idea is cultivate the good feeling experience.

Here is a quick three step prosperity method that also works... 1. List out all of your goals and put dates by them. 2. Visualize your goals. 3. Be bold in affirming your goals (Ponder, C. *The Dynamic Laws of Prosperity*).

If you have problems with prosperity on an individual basis... this will not serve you in business or a leadership position very well. Determine to work on your prosperity mindset now. For additional help with your prosperity mindset, check out my audio program at a substantial discount here:

http://www.lifeisjoyful.org/prosperity.html

*****

Personal Story

Your Emotions are Your Power to Your Prosperity

By Hemal Radia, Law of Attraction Expert

For many people, when they are trying to attract prosperity, they do not yet see themselves with what they want and hence do not find it easy to attract it.

I remember around 16 years ago when I was first learning about manifesting and visualizing, I visualized a computer that I wanted at the time. I had done this visualizing on a Tuesday or Wednesday and that Friday I happened to be in a meeting with a company director and he offered me one of their computers.

You'd think that that was it and I had my computer? It was not quite like that. He offered me a computer and it was one which was a very old one and not feasible to be used anymore. So, I put my intention back 'out there' and trusted it would be taken care of.

That lunchtime I passed a computer store and picked up one of their brochures and went for lunch in a nearby restaurant. As I read the brochure, on the back page I saw an offer for a computer which was just perfect and it had an interest-free credit arrangement which was just perfect for me at the time! Within a short period of time the computer and I were together exactly how I had envisioned it.

How is this any different from attracting any other type of 'prosperity'? It's not any different. It's the same thing. If you can clearly see yourself with what you want (or at least not have an issue with clearly seeing yourself with what you want), you are more likely to attract it.

The clarity that you envision is an indicator of a clear vibration you are offering the Universe for what you want. If you feel resistance about it or uncomfortable when you think about it, there are aspects to turn your attention away from, and towards what you DO want.

When you are clearly aligned to what you want – and you will know this because you will be heading towards having the full-body excitement and anticipation for it, you won't be having to 'think' about what you want, because you will be so in your moment and heading towards it. You will be living your now.

Envision what you want as clearly and powerfully and vividly as you can. The greater the emotion and more 'real' that it feels, the more powerful your vibration is in pulling in what you want. Regularly work on building this feeling to a better and better and more 'real' place. You will find along the way that you will have manifestations that occur, or you can just enjoy the happening of that which you want when it happens in its entirety.

Know that you and what you want are on your way to meeting...

Hemal Radia

Hemal Radia is the Author of "Find You, And You Find Everything: The Secrets to the Law of Attraction." He is a world-renowned expert on Manifesting & Law of Attraction. http://www.hemalradia.com

*****

I adore Hemal's work. He clearly shows the power of vibration in relationship to prosperity with this story. He also demonstrates that we can practice the law of attraction on every day, smaller goals. It is not the size of the goal, but how you feel about it.

Exercise:

Practice these prosperity affirmations- say each three times and repeat a few times per day:

50 Affirmations on Prosperity by Sheri Kaye Hoff

1. I now receive all of my good.
2. I am open to receive, now.
3. I am now open to my good coming to me as a divine surprise.
4. The Universe has the "way"- I come up with the "what".
5. Abundance is all around me all of the time.
6. I open my heart and mind to see abundance.
7. I now appreciate my life.
8. I appreciate my rich blessings from the Universe.
9. I appreciate everyone around me.
10. I see everyone as worthy to be blessed and prospered.
11. I bless and prosper everyone.
12. I have the courage to see my dreams.
13. I now have the skills, knowledge, and resources to achieve my dreams.
14. I am living the life of my dreams.
15. Money is a blessing.

16. I am a terrific money manager.
17. Money comes to me easily, often, and from many channels.
18. I choose the best.
19. Money is divine substance.
20. I am genius when it comes to managing my money.
21. Every time I give…I receive.
22. I give generously.
23. I now pay all of my bills with joy and love.
24. I think big.
25. I am now capable of greatness.
26. My heart sings with joy.
27. Everything is always working out for me.
28. My plans work out.
29. I easily attract great opportunities, now.
30. The right people come into my life.
31. The people in my life are now supportive.
32. I have time for the important people in my life.
33. My time spent with others is now filled with fun and laughter.
34. I act when the path is revealed.
35. I confidently speak my truth.
36. I easily discern my life's purpose.
37. I am committed to the purpose of my life.

38. I am aligned with my purpose.
39. I am energized and refreshed by my purpose.
40. Passionate work energizes me.
41. I am now passionate about life and my work.
42. I easily make the best choices for me and the highest good.
43. I feel prosperous every moment of every day.
44. I take excellent care of my body.
45. I make time for fun.
46. Being organized in every aspect of my life comes easily and naturally to me.
47. I am on time and have perfect timing in my life.
48. I now release all limiting beliefs including those beneath the surface of my consciousness.
49. I prosper and thrive, now.
50. Prosperity is a beautiful gift that I lovingly receive, now.

CHAPTER 6: I-I LOVE

"Let us not be satisfied with just giving money. Money is not enough, money can be got, but they need your hearts to love them. So, spread your love everywhere you go." - **Mother Teresa**

The next piece of the acronym, INSPIRE is the second I- I-love. I have decided that I would not ever teach any leadership course without bringing in the concept of unconditional love. It is that important and often overlooked. I do not mean that you walk around work hugging people, telling them that you love them. However, you could be thinking it inside. Practicing unconditional love involves a state of being and a commitment, rather than announcing- "I am practicing unconditional love". Be love.

I do have a deep love for my team; I have a deep love for myself. You have to love yourself deeply in order to love others effectively.

Almost every situation (at work, at home) could be improved by adding more love. I am not talking about romantic love between partners. I am talking about a deep love- unconditional love- as a verb- an act- instead of a feeling.

One way to effectively implement unconditional love involves anytime you have a conflict. Ask, "What would it look like if I added more love here?" Just your being in a state of love, impacts other people. Unconditional love is the strongest energy vibration on the planet. If you think practicing love is a weak approach... think about this- people have no defense against you if you have a heart full of love. An example of this is Gandhi's civil disobedience in India and his whole movement. His movement turned into a global movement of peace, love, and non-violence.

Though you might not be a civil rights leader, you can practice unconditional love as part of your leadership practice. If you walk into a room and you are full of love for life and everyone in it, people just kind of melt around you. It is an incredible power and power for good.

Recognize that practicing unconditional love is more powerful, than if you approach a situation and you are angry and yelling at people telling them everything that they are doing wrong. When you bring love- you create comfort and a trust environment. People are free to express their innate talents and creativity.

Your people do not have to know that you are walking around, just loving them. But they might actually understand on a vibrational and intuitive level what you are doing.

Concentrate on bringing love to every possible situation in your life and note the changes that occur as a result.

You might be thinking, it is hard to feel loving when I am angry, under pressure, upset, or things are going wrong. Here is where you look at love as more than a feeling. You decide it is your desired state of being. Act with love and the feeling will follow it.

Implementing unconditional love is part of being a transformational leader. When you are a transformational leader, your people become better- they transform beyond any expectations. Performance increases exponentially and sometimes inexplicably. Everyone is on board and feels like they are part of something larger than themselves.

Synergistic results unfold.

Here is a quick exercise that you can use to feel more love at anytime. Put your hand over your heart and leave it there for several minutes. Try it.

Exercise:

Transformational Leadership Quiz

Rate yourself 1- 10 for each criterion.

- When I work with people, their performances increase.
- People seem to follow me easily.
- People resonate with my message.
- My goals are for the highest good of all.
- I build high trust relationships.
- The people around me sense that I care.
- I get to know what is important to other people.
- I set a great example.
- I handle difficult situations with ease.
- I praise lavishly.

- I give honest feedback.

Journal prompts:

Transformational Leadership means to me...

What do I need to do to be a truly transformational leader?

CHAPTER 7: R- REACHING OUT

*"The highest of distinctions is service to others." –*King George VI

Reaching Out is the next part of the INSPIRE acronym. When you are reaching out: you are deciding where you are going to make the difference; what is important to you; who do you want to reach? Where is your impact? Where is your circle of influence?

Decide where you are going to make a difference. Maybe your impact will be in your neighborhood, your community, your city, or even the globe. If you have a business you might call this discovering your niche.

Make your choices on how you are going to make a difference. For instance, I consciously make the choice in my life that everyone I meet- gets 100% of me. I want to make an impact in the quality of life on a global basis. I do this through my books that I have written, my audio programs, and my coaching programs. When I wrote my first book, I never imagined that I would write multiple books and I did not imagine that I would have a global reach. Now a global impact is part of my annual plans. I feel so blessed to be able to reach people. Every time I hear about one heart being inspired, I feel encouraged to keep going. When I feel tired at times, an email will come in sharing a story and I get energized again. Each day is an opportunity to recommit.

Sometimes the impact we make comes from being gentle and friendly, by refusing to get mad.

My kids laugh at me because I have this thing where I will not honk my horn at anybody when I am driving for any reason, except when I am just about to get killed by their car. If someone is changing lanes and they are an inch away from my car, I maybe will honk the horn- but most of the time, I will not honk my horn. I know that I have cut people off by accident, so I do not feel like I have to punish every single person who ever cuts me off when I am driving.

Your difference could be that you are going to be and live a certain way and your example will impact other people.

You could make a difference by committing to keep your word.

You have the opportunity to reach out and make a difference no matter what the circumstances are in your life.

Remember that you are not alone even if you work in a cubicle or even if you work at your computer all day. If you are a writer and you only talk to your publisher once a month or even less than that, you are still not alone, you still need other people. If you are a writer and you publish books, you need people to buy your books, right? So whether you recognize it or not, you are reaching people, through the words that you write and you are touching a part of their soul. Even though you might be thinking there is distance between me and that person, you are still connecting.

Reach out and give generously of your time and your resources, make it a point to lift other people up. If there is a member on your team struggling, grab that person and lift them up. Help them along. Stop and help someone with their groceries. You get the idea. So start. If you are already reaching out- expand.

Once you begin reaching out, then expanding your reach, choose meaningful impact instead of dabbling around. It's much more effective for you to be heavily involved in one or two or three or even four things than to try to do 50 things. Decide that you are going to make a meaningful difference.

Journal prompt:

What will a meaningful difference look like for you?

One often overlooked part of reaching out is the ability to receive as well give. Imagine that you are reaching out and you are helping other people, you are lifting people up, you are making a difference- then, let people give to you.

How do you receive the good that is coming to you? Do you close yourself off from it? Do you ask people for help when you need it or do you sit there and wonder why no one is helping you or do you refuse help?

When you refuse help, you are not allowing other people to have the pleasure of giving. You are, in effect, taking away one of life's great pleasures from them.

I would like to challenge you in this area of receiving. This week, practice asking for help or practice receiving an unexpected gift. If someone gives you something unexpectedly, do not run out and figure out what you have to give them - just say thank you. Gracefully receive those unexpected gifts.

Use affirmations like- *I am open to receive.*

When you are in the reaching out phase, you are in a circle of life, you are giving, yet you are also receiving. If you can imagine light circulating around the planet, going out to other people and coming back to you, and you are not disrupting that light, you are part of that glow- the abundant flow of the universe.

*****

Personal Story

Learn to be More Caring and Compassionate

By Connie Nylund

"Service is the rent we pay for being. It is the very purpose of life, and not something you do

*in your spare time." –Marian Wright
Edelman, a children's activist.*

*One of the best things we can do for our health
is to learn to be more caring and
compassionate. – says Stephen Post, director
of the Center for Medical Humanities,
Compassionate Care and Bioethics, at Stony
Brook University in New York. "Happiness is
a byproduct of living generously." He
referenced a study in the journal SCIENCE,
2008, where a group of 600 men and women
participated to find out how personal spending
was related to happiness. Personal spending
was found to be unrelated to happiness. On
the other hand, pro-social spending, on gifts to
others and donations to charities, was directly
related to happiness.*

*There seems to be a very enthusiastic nod of
approval for people who volunteer. Studies on
volunteer habits of people show that
volunteerism showed the largest increase
between 2008 and 2009 after a decline
following 2002. Volunteers are generally
young, female, home owners, those who do not
have to commute long distances, and many
volunteers work fulltime. With studies
showing people can benefit physically and
psychologically as they age by from
volunteering 1-2 hours a week, there may be
more efforts to recruit volunteers from the
older population. Important to note:
Volunteering too many hours has the*

*deleterious effect of reducing or even
eliminating the benefits.*

*To personalize the value of volunteering, John
Nylund, Sheri's father, has provided some
examples from his 31 year career in
corrections and his 12 years of retirement. As
the Education Director at a correctional
facility, John worked with a staff complement
of 4 classroom teachers with basic ed., 1
driver's ed. and phys ed. instructor, 1 floating
sub, and 1 science teacher.*

*John frequently filled in as needed in the
classroom, on wilderness treks, and
supervising other activities. His ethic was to
do what needed to be done. He went above
and beyond and made time to personally talk
with the boys and encourage them. John went
fishing, camping, canoeing, hiking, rock
climbing, cross country and downhill skiing,
year round. He packed supplies, cooked,
paddled, swam, brought youth to the doctor
and dentist, chased runaways, defended,
restrained, consoled, joked, played baseball,
you name it.*

*Over the years, John has found many success
stories among the graduates. Some went
home to attend public school, some graduated
at camp and went to college or the military.
Some went to prestigious universities. Some
became policemen, firemen, social workers,
construction workers, businessmen. Some got
married and had families. Some came to live*

by faith. One young man John remembers became a counselor in anger management for victims and perpetrators. How did this happen? He was such a volatile youth. Well, one last outburst and one of the arresting police officers was angrier than He was, yelling, "Let me at him. Let me at him!" He realized he had to change, and he did.

After retiring, John started mentoring youth at church. He took the boys hunting, target shooting, and fishing, and they read the Bible together and did their confirmation lessons. Over the years some of the boys and their parents have updated John on what they are doing. Education. Careers. Family life. The cycle continues. Now John is involved with substitute teaching for the teen class at church and still praying for young men, for their faith to unfold and lead them to a desire to serve God by serving others.

Connie Nylund

English Teacher and Blogger

*****

If you haven't realized yet, John is my father, and Connie is my blogging mom. It is only fitting that the earliest influencers of my path would be a part of this book today. I have always thought that my father was the busiest retired person I had ever known. You would think that after all of those years of service making a difference in troubled youths' lives during his career, he would say, "I have done enough", yet he still serves out of the joy and passion he has in his heart.

*****

Personal Story

Everyone is Perfect and Powerful!

Nanice Ellis

One beautiful summer night in 1987, I left the Actor's Institute in New York City and headed home to Long Island. I passed by a homeless woman lying asleep in a doorway. I did not have much cash with me, but I felt strongly that I should leave something anyway. I put some bills in the sleeping woman's hand and walked away. Then, I realized that I had depleted my cab fare and, in fact, only had enough money left to take the Long Island railroad. That meant a long, late night walk to Penn Station in four inch high heels.

After a few blocks and a developing blister, I decided to take off my shoes and walk barefoot the rest of the way. Since it was a warm, clear night it did not seem like anything could stop me from enjoying the walk.

It had not yet occurred to me that the path I had chosen to walk to Penn Station would lead me through some less desirable areas. Just as I was passing by a burned out building, I noticed a large gang watching me from across the street. There was no one else around and the seriousness of the situation quickly became apparent. The gang crossed the street at an angle clearly intended to cut me off. I felt fear flow through me. My pulse quickened. Everything told me that this was not going to be good.

But then something shifted inside me. I remembered who they really were; intrinsically powerful beings playing the part of thugs because they had forgotten their own true power. The gang surrounded me matching my pace. I focused on the leader who had moved in and was walking beside me. Looking him straight in the eye; I smiled and said, "What a beautiful night – do not you think?" Dead silence. No response from anyone. The gang waited for a cue from him. No one made a sound for what seemed like much longer than the few seconds it really was. I continued to walk, smiling up at him. Finally, the leader said "What's a good-lookin' girl like you doin' walking these streets alone? Don't you know how dangerous that is?" Then he insisted that he and his gang walk me all the way to Penn Station so that they could protect me.

By remembering my own intrinsic power and separating the behaviors of this gang from the intrinsically powerful beings I knew they really were; my potential attackers became my protectors – my enemies became my friends – and a potentially violent and destructive situation shifted into a positive empowering one for everyone involved.

As we recognize our inherent perfection and personal power, we are led to the natural conclusion that others are likewise amazing souls with equal inherent and intrinsic worth and power – even if, in the moment, they are acting otherwise. When we accept any environment into which we are led and pay attention to every soul within that environment; and when we treat them with respect and appreciation for who they really are; we create a larger space for possibilities of powerful positive connection even – especially – with the opposition. We help them recognize or at least feel their true power and make different choices even in the most unlikely of circumstances.

When others sense our acknowledgment and appreciation of who they really are and our comfortable connection with them, the results are amazing. Even in conflict or other apparently "adverse" circumstances, when we pay more attention to the people than to the conflict, productive and profitable relationships are often established with the "opposition."

What will happen to you in your relationships when you recognize not only your own, but other's intrinsic power and perfection? It only takes one person in a relationship to shift the relationship in profound ways. What would happen if that one person was you? How might you be able to shift even the worst relationship into one that supports everyone involved? You, and only you, have the power to create the kind of relationships you want and deserve.

From the book, "The Infinite Power of YOU!
By Nanice Ellis
www.Nanice.com

*****

Nanice shares a great story about reaching out and making a difference. I love her courage, wisdom, and strength.

For leaders, business people, consultants, and managers, expanding your reach must be intentional and this is the area that impacts the number of clients, the number of sales- your bottom line.

I have included the Expand Your Reach Assessment exercise to help you assess where your business or practice is right now and then to help you set goals for growth. You can also use this to assess your professional network if you work for an organization.

Exercise:

Expand Your Reach Assessment:

1- What is the size of your email list?
2- What is your social media reach (facebook, twitter, and LinkedIn)?
3- What is your blogging subscriber list and your frequency of blogging?
4- When is the last time you met someone new?
5- Do you know someone on every continent?
6- What is your niche? No niche? No problem- what do you like doing?
7- Where can you find people in your niche/or areas of interest?

8- What are you currently doing to grow your email list/social media reach?

9- Do you have a list management process in place?

10- Who do you consider to be part of your inner circle?

11- When is the last time you attended a live event? Who did you meet when you were there?

12- Identify support people you need (e.g. an agent, a marketing specialist, a coach, etc)

Set goals for the following:

- Social media:
- Email list:
- Face to Face interaction:
- Charitable organizations:
- Business Growth: Sales? Number of clients? Number of products (what kind of products)
- Career growth: Promotion opportunities? Training opportunities? a new position?, etc

CHAPTER 8: E- MANAGING YOUR ENERGY AND ENTHUSIASM

Do not pray for tasks equal to your powers; pray for powers equal to your tasks."- Phillips Brooks, bishop and orator (1835-1893)

The last part of the INSPIRE acronym is E-managing your energy and enthusiasm. You need balance in your life with attention given to all three areas- mind, body, spirit. Most of us have one area that fails a little bit. If you notice an area of struggle- get a coach to help you through so you can experience an energy balance.

Your energy level affects your ability to attract what you want in life. You want to have a high energy vibration so you can attract the highest and best to you and your people.

Learn to become self-aware. Recognize common energy drains:

- Incompletions
- "Shoulds"
- Not speaking your truth
- Clutter
- Procrastination
- Sedentary lifestyle
- Too many stimulants, etc

Here are some simple energy shifting exercises:

- Complete one task that is hanging over your head.
- Organize a file or dresser drawer.
- Walk around the block
- Do one item that is part of a large project
- Say, I love you and/or I forgive you.

Your energy and enthusiasm in your life brings everything together- your energy makes life work or it makes life get really tough.

Your goal is to have an energy balance in your life between mind, body and spirit. You can do a check-in right now on how you are doing and why do not you give yourself three separate ratings: for mind – your mental energy, how clear is your mindset? How positive are you?

Do you feel mentally alert? Rate yourself on a scale of 1 -10, 10 being the highest.

Next —the body: how physically healthy do you feel? Do you have energy? Do you wake up and have enough energy to get started and get through your day? Do you mostly feel energized, strong, flexible, and fit? Rate yourself on a scale of 1 to 10.

And then, what about spirituality? Do you feel like you have a clear conscience? Do you feel like you have a spiritual connection? Rate yourself on a scale of 1- 10.

Let's look at the energy drains.

One of the biggies is incompletion. Consider whether or not you have a multitude of incomplete things hanging over your head. Maybe you have a stack of bills that you haven't opened; maybe there are repairs that need to be done in your home; maybe there is car maintenance; maybe there are meetings that you postponed. That feeling of being incomplete often seems to suck the life out of a person and it adds to overwhelm.

The next energy drain is all the "shoulds" we place on ourselves:

- I should be exercising;
- I should be looking for a better job;
- I should make more money
- I should be nice to this person; etc.

"I should be" – whatever. Many of us have long, laundry lists of "shoulds" that make us feel like failures and that we never measure up to a certain standard. Think about all of the "shoulds" that you have in your own personal story.

Everyone has their list of shoulds. Check in and see what kind of shoulds you have in your life. Oftentimes, when we think of the word *should*, we can almost hear our mothers' voices. And the *should* usually arises from someone else's goal and we resist it. That's why it's a *should*, instead of an *I want to* or, *I am doing"* or, *I am going to do.*

A *should* could also be an unrealistic expectation that we have of ourselves. Change your expectation in your life to doing the things that you want to do- the things that are deeply important to you and align with your core values.

If you are continuing your education because you feel like it's something you should do, this is completely different than continuing your education because it's something of interest and passion for you.

If you accept a promotion at work because you just think it's the next logical step in something you should do, it's different than really wanting that promotion and being excited about it.

Another big energy drain is not speaking your truth.

When you are going through life not speaking your truth or you say, "Everything's okay" or "That's okay," or "That doesn't matter", or, "No big deal." you drain your energy. Make a commitment to speak your truth and speaking your truth doesn't mean you have to be argumentative and it doesn't have to make someone else wrong.

If you do not want to do something, make it about the fact that you do not want to do it, not that the other person is so awful for asking.

If you really want to go somewhere, if you are planning a vacation and you have strong feelings, speak your truth. If you are in a meeting and someone says something really upsetting, find a way to speak your truth. You can still be gentle with your truth. You could say, "Your comments made me uncomfortable." You do not have to raise your voice; you do not have to make a scene; you can just speak your truth.

One of the things that I remember really well about living at home with my Dad is he had no problems saying no. If he did not want to do something, he would just say, "no" and he did not explain why, it was just *no*, and his voice did not rise, he was not angry. He did not feel like he had to explain and I do not think anyone ever really asked him to explain.

Sometimes when we are trying to speak our truth, we back-pedal into it. You can be empowered to clearly say, "This is the truth for me," and recognize that it is your truth. Your truth can be different from another person's truth. You could both be right. Own your truth and your energy will skyrocket.

The next thing that is a big energy drainer is clutter; and if you do not think that's true, clean up some clutter and notice how you feel once you do.

Keeping things from the past is not something that is energy-productive. For instance, if you have a collection of boxes in your basement or your garage and you have not touched them or gone through them in years, essentially you have dead energy sitting there.

There are things that we keep for the memories, - scrapbooks, photos, memorabilia- and we may not look through them on a regular basis. However, a lot of what we keep, we do not even know why we keep it. Tidy things up, get rid of things, organize- and you will feel an instant boost in your energy.

Procrastination is another huge energy drain. If you are constantly delaying and putting things off —this habit pulls and sucks the energy right out of you.

If you have been putting something off and not addressing the issues, ask, "Could I just make even a small start on this? Will I see a boost in it in energy if I just start on this project? What if I could do one thing towards to getting it done?"

Another thing that is a large energy drain is a sedentary lifestyle. If you sit mostly for work and then you sit for your entertainment through the television or the computer and you are never outside, you are never moving your body; you will not feel very energetic. So the antidote to that, of course, is to move your body

But one of the things that people do is they say, "Oh, I've got to exercise; I've got to join a gym. And when am I going to find time to do it and what gym am I going to join?" Truthfully- you could just walk around the block. Ten minutes of moving your body is enough to get your energy to lift.

Moving your body can include things like getting up and stretching; or doing some push-ups against your dresser. When you move your body, try to do things that move your entire body. Try dance, zumba, or yoga. Look through magazines or surf the internet for ideas on how to move your body.

I was listening to a speaker who was in her 70's. She said when she was growing up, people did not talk about exercise, they moved. They did real activities and they had fun. They went for walks and they had fun. They rode bikes and they had fun. They did not say, "Oh, I have to get my 30 minutes of cardio in," If you can take yourself back to doing things, moving your body because it is fun this will also be a boost for your energy.

Another energy drain is too many stimulants and this could be medication that you are taking, it could be coffee, it could even be television, too much sugar, too many carbs. Then, we get exhausted and have a hard time settling down. Jittery energy is not positive energy.

You may want to get a nutritionist involved and be sure to pick a nutritionist who is focused on the quality of foods that you eat instead of calories. There is a big difference between eating a low calorie diet and eating a diet with high quality foods.

I have some simple energy shifting exercises that you can do and you could keep a list handy so that when you feel low, you can try one of these instead of reaching for a doughnut or that fourth or fifth cup of coffee.

The first one is to complete one task that is hanging over your head and what I would love for you to do right now is write one down. Write down one task that you commit to doing over the next week.

Organize a file or dresser drawer. I like this one because it is simple and contained. If I said, "Organize your closet," for some people who can barely shut their closet door that might be completely overwhelming. If you look at one drawer or one file, that is something that could be completed in a short window of time.

Here is a little prosperity tip to go along with the dresser-drawer activity- leave one drawer empty and the same with a closet- leave one closet shelf empty. When you create room for something new, then that something new will appear in your life.

The next energy boosting suggestion is to do one item that's part of a large project. I'll give you a book example. Instead of looking at the entire project, start by making an outline or gathering resources, or writing the first paragraph.

Another example: If you are looking for a job, maybe your one item that is part of a large project might be to do some internet searches on jobs that are available in your area or jobs that are interesting to you in any area.

An additional example of doing one item to help your job search might be to revamp your resume. Everyone, even if you own your own business, should always have a current resume. Revisit your resume at least quarterly, or even monthly. Make sure that you look at that resume and update it regularly. Here is what typically happens: someone gets a job and then they are in place for a year or two years. When they decide that they want to look for another job, that's when they think about their resume and realize that they have extensive revisions to do to update it.

 Maintain your positive career and work energy by keeping your resume organized and updated. This is a sign that you are always ready for the next career opportunity. You could make it a point to add to your resume every time you accomplish something. If you earn a promotion, if you complete training, if you win an award – anything that you want to add to your resume, you could add it as it happens. Make sure that you keep your resume document backed up, too· have a copy on your computer, a copy on your email, an external hard drive or jump drive, and then in online storage somewhere.

The next energy boosting activity: say, "I love you," and/or "I forgive you,"· which will boost your energy immediately. This works even if the words are said to your dog or cat

Each day people say or do things that can make us a little bit crazy or irritated. What do we typically do about it? Oftentimes we go on and on with negative thoughts: "Oh I can't believe no one took the trash out; I can't believe that the neighbor parked their car in my spot," and resentment builds.

Mentally think, "I forgive you," for all of these small irritations and you will free and clear your energy.

There is a Hawaiian principle called ho'oponopono based on these four statements:
- I love you,
- I am sorry,
- Please forgive me,
- Thank you.

You can use these statements as a mantra to clear and clean your energy. Of these four statements, in my experience, people sometimes have problems with the *I am sorry* part. This is true especially if people have been in terrible abusive relationships and they feel like they should not have to apologize in any way.

I look at the statement *I am sorry* as I am sorry for whatever piece I had in the whole scope of the universe in creating any of my issues that I have today.

I view the statement *please forgive me* as please forgive me to the whole universe. You are asking for forgiveness, for anything that you have done that got in the way of your own or anyone else's highest good – clearing and cleaning out any negative energy.

And the *I love you* and *thank you* are self-explanatory and some people like to use simply, "thank you, thank you, thank you..." as their mantra and that's fine too because being full of appreciation and gratitude is a gigantic boost to energy.

Try the ho'oponopono Hawaiian principle. It has been discussed by Dr. Hew Len and Dr. Joe Vitale in a book called *Zero-Limits*. It's an ancient principle. Try it and see what happens.

Most often I feel an instant energy shift when I say the four sentences over and over again.

If you feel like you are in a toxic environment at work or anywhere, try using these statements to make an energetic shift for not just you but for everybody.

Make an effort to keep your energy and the energy of your team and family high. Clear, clean, and boost often.

Create your own list of activities that you can use to shift your energy. Then, when you need it, you will have ideas at your fingertips.

*****

Personal Story:

Your Personal Energy is a Precious Resource

By Linda L. Hardenstein, MPA, PCC

If you are a high-powered career woman you probably know what it's like to be a road warrior, traveling extensively, working hard to stay a step ahead of the competition, taking it all on to survive in a lean and mean environment. I lived this life. I was full of drive, commitment, push and I could accomplish a lot. What I did not realize was it couldn't last.

After two back-to-back cross country business flights and an exhausting schedule I fell down a flight of 18 steps on the way to an early morning meeting. Rolling down the stairs I heard a voice say, "I could be breaking my neck right now." Months of rehab and physical therapy forced me to live my life differently and gave me time to think about my choices and my energy.

My fall was a wake-up call. But I'd been hooked on the adrenaline of the rat race for years. What if I lost an opportunity because I slowed down and actually had a life? I did not even know the steps to take to do it differently. That small inner voice kept saying, "You'd better change." I gave myself a new mission – to learn the secret to mastering my energy and to owning my life. Being a coach, I wanted to teach others who were trapped in the same kind of lifestyle what I learned on my journey, such as:

Energy is precious. It not guaranteed nor is there an unending supply. It has to be generated. Think of the tumultuous waters that power the turbines to generate electricity in a hydro-electric power plant. Physical movement, eating well, drinking water and getting enough rest, powers up your energy level and generates the steam that gets you through your day.

Energy must be sustained. Our physical environment impacts us more than we realize. What you surround yourself with either sustains you or drains you. To sustain your energy surround yourself with the things you *love – pictures of loved ones, flowers on your desk, a poster of your dream travel destination. Clutter blocks your energy. Clear it and it will open new space in your life. You know that sparkle you feel when you clean your space? That's energy! If people are dragging you down and cluttering your life, consider clearing them out too!*

Energy must be renewed. Do you know what your rejuvenator is? My clients learn to identify their rejuvenators because without them, stress and overwhelm can run rampant. Your rejuvenator is usually something you do that is totally different from who you really are, or who you think you should be in the world.

For example, if you are a straight-laced, suit-wearing professional like an attorney, your rejuvenator might be riding your Harley over the weekend. If you are someone who works with people all week, like a Realtor or a retail sales clerk, you might rejuvenate by reading a book at home alone or taking time out to meditate. It is that activity or non-activity that renews you.

Your personal energy is a precious resource to be treasured, generated, sustained and renewed.

Making a conscious decision to be the master of your own life means you take responsibility for managing your energy, which in turn can transform you life into a richer, more balance and fulfilling experience.

Linda Hardenstein, MPA, PCC

Your Achievement Partner

www.lindahardenstein.com

*****

Your enthusiasm is also incredibly important…to you and to your business/career/team. Think of this story- imagine that you are trying to buy a shirt and someone says, "oh yeah there are shirts over there on the table, you can take a look." Or if, instead, someone says, "we just received these 100% cotton t-shirts and they are in such vibrant colors, and we just marked them down 25% today, here let me show you." Totally different, right?

Commit to enthusiasm in whatever you are doing. Be excited about it. You want to bubble over and ooze sincere enthusiasm…

If you are shy, you can still be enthusiastic. Your enthusiasm will just be expressed in a different way than an outgoing person would express enthusiasm. People have different ways of being enthusiastic. But you need to cultivate it and show enthusiasm to the world and your team because people naturally follow people who are excited about life. It feels good to be enthusiastic. I know that I feel good when I am acting with enthusiasm.

And another way to keep your enthusiasm up is to praise generously and choose words carefully when criticizing.

Frequently remind yourself why you are doing what you are doing so you can keep up your enthusiastic outlook.

I get really excited and enthusiastic and I have been that way for my whole life. I wave my arms, I jump up and down. I even do a cartwheel every year just to make sure I can still do one. Now, my husband is different, the most enthusiastic thing he ever says is, "Oh, that's good," and that is his version of doing back flips. When I told him I was pregnant with our first child, he said, "Congratulations". (I almost thought he was going to shake my hand).

Okay, so people are different and you cannot expect a very quiet introspective person to suddenly do backhand springs and be jumping up and down screaming. However, I have seen introverted people give key-note speeches and create artificial enthusiasm that actually works, and this is how they do it- they approach it from a physical perspective. They might be back-stage jumping up and down, stretching, beating on their chests. They get the blood pumping through their bodies. When they get on stage, they exhibit more enthusiasm.

Even really enthusiastic people are not enthusiastic all the time.

I find myself at times having to do some chest pumping and some jumping jacks to get really enthusiastic if I feel like my energy is a little bit low or if I feel a bit distracted.

It is also, okay if you have a quieter, gentler level of enthusiasm. You need to show enthusiasm in your own way to the world and your team because people want to naturally follow people who are excited about life and possibilities.

Think about it this way: if you were to walk into a store and you were looking for bedding and someone said, "Oh yeah, there's some bedding over there. Why do not you go, take a look at it," or someone says, "Yes, we just got in gorgeous comforters, come over and take a look, feel it, sit down, on the bed, feel what it feels like, lie down on the bed, in fact."

Can you tell that I am enthusiastic about shopping?

I am not talking about the crazy used cars salesman kind of pep. I mean genuine enthusiasm. If you want people to get on board with you, you have to be enthusiastic. Be enthusiastic about what you are doing and if you do not have any enthusiasm about what you are doing, maybe you need to be doing something else.

If you are a waiter and you want to be a singer, I am not suggesting that you quit your job if you have bills to pay.

And if you decided, "Okay, I have a singing career and a singing career is important to me, but it is also important to me to be enthusiastic at my waiter job, because I know that I need my job right now in order to pay my bills; so, when I am there, I am going put everything into it."

You can make up your mind to do that too. If you are not enthusiastic about your job, either make up your mind to be enthusiastic or find something else to do.

One effective way that you can foster enthusiasm is to praise generously. Think about how people are with grandchildren, or little small children or puppies. A puppy goes outside to the bathroom for the first time and you are so excited, you exclaim, "It's so great! Good job, good job, puppy."

Or your child takes his first steps or your child says his first words and you think he is the most brilliant person on the planet. People are very generous with praise in these examples, but we need to keep praising generously throughout our lifetimes.

There's an expression, *catch someone doing something right,*" instead of catching someone doing something wrong. What about deliberately looking for the good with your employees, your coworkers? If you started each day intentionally trying to find them doing something really well, how will that shift your day and their days? And think about applying this with your spouse, your children, your significant other, and /or your partner.

If you started the day and you could actually find a way to praise people first · What if your first words each day could be praising generously. What a shift! What a life-changing shift!
However, there are times when you have to say something was done incorrectly. Find a way to be gentle about it. Avoid making people feel like terrible people because they make a mistake. Explain the mistake; explain what

needs to change and then move on. It is also helpful to affirm the relationship as the conversation is ending.

Another way to boost your enthusiasm is to read motivational literature. Always have a good book ·on your Kindle, next to your bed, in your handbag, in your car· have something positive that you can read that is going to pick you up.

I love quotes because they are short and you can ponder them for a while. I have quotes up all over my home and office. Wherever I look· I see a quote.

Create a toolbox. Put some motivational literature into what I call your tool box. In your tool box, you will want to keep all of the motivational tools you need to keep you going on the path that you want to follow...

The next piece of being enthusiastic is hanging out with other enthusiastic people. Yes! Do not hang out with depressed, sad people. I am not saying abandon your friends who are experiencing grief, but please make sure to be around positive, uplifting people, too. Be around other people who are enthusiastic· people who look at life as the glass is half full, people who see the good in life. And if you do not have friends like that, go find some. You probably noticed if you hang out with people who say, "Oh the economy is so tough," or,

"Politicians are so crooked," and they have a negative view of life, you find yourself to be utterly exhausted.

Instead, hang out with people who are doers, who are movers, who are shakers, who are achievers; they always have something going on even if they are 90 years old. They are excited about life.

I remember when my grandmother was sick; she would still be excited about a card game.

I remember my grandmother being hooked up to oxygen and still jumping rope in the backyard. I have no idea how she made that work but I remember it vividly· seeing my grandma jump rope with oxygen tubing in her nose and an oxygen tank fairly close by.

Watch videos of inspiring speakers. Conduct an internet search for inspiring speakers. If you want to know some names of people: how about Tony Robbins; Bryan Tracy; Zig Ziglar, Joel Osteen, Steven Covey, Louise Hay, Cheryl Richardson, Wayne Dyer, Doreen Virtue...other favorites?

You can also find meditations on the internet. In fact when I was still teaching college classes, I would be up so late grading papers, and then I would be wound up. In order to relax I would find monks chanting on the internet and I would lean back in my chair, listen, and close my eyes.

You can find anything that you need to feed your soul in any particular moment and keep your focus on the zest for life and not ever be focused on just getting by.

Sometimes we wake up and we think, "Let's see if it's going to be an okay day. I can make it through it." No, no, no, we want to do more than just make it through we want to have that zest for life. We want to have that spark - that something exciting; that something that makes us get goose bumps.

Take a moment and consider this: When I say zest for life, what do you think of? What comes to mind? Write down two or three ideas.

For me what comes to mind is the Caribbean. I love the Caribbean. When I am in the water, in a lagoon or on the beach enjoying a pina colada; and I can't see a skyscraper anywhere, I feel so calm, yet energized.

Another special place for me is Grizzly Bear Creek located in the Rocky Mountains along I-70. There is a little waterfall and the water is always cool even when the sun is really hot. I like to sit there and put my feet in the water. It's a beautiful little place- part of my zest for life.

Another way that I experience my zest for life happens every single day. I bring my son to school. Then, I get coffee. When I am coming back from the coffee shop and I turn the corner, the view I see is snow-capped, sparkling pink mountain peaks, because the sun is rising and it turns the snow kind of pink and lavender-y. It sparkles and it takes my breath away every single day when I see it. My heart fills with appreciation.

You are meant to experience the zest.

Another tip for developing your enthusiasm: trying new things and learning something new. When we exercise our brains, we get a valuable enthusiasm shake up and perhaps even new ideas about business or careers.

Another piece of being enthusiastic is being an action taker. What do I mean by that? You learn something new – implement it. Do not just think about things – act.

When I learned how to create movies, I did not say, "Oh, that's good to know." I did it. I created videos. I took action and that boosts enthusiasm.

Develop a mantra for yourself.

It could be, *Be BOLD* or *Be the Inspiration* (my mantras) or *Be Strong, Be the Change –*

whatever it is for you, have a saying that you say to yourself whenever you need that boost.

When you create your annual plan, use a slogan for the year – so when you do not feel like doing anything or you feel like you are not seeing progress, you can use the mantra as motivation. If you lead other people, you might even have a slogan that can be unifying and rallying.

*****

Personal Story:

Enthusiasm Found!

By Janet Nestor, Energy Psychologist

My childhood was often challenging and filled with fear. There was a lot of stress, and I did not like it. I wanted something different. I did not know how to create what I wanted, but I made a conscious decision to live a full and happy adult life.

My transformational journey accelerated when I was about thirty years old and in graduate school. I had very young children, little understanding of emotional balance and no insight into energetic self-care. Eager for change, I knew I had a lot to learn. I met Dr. Premala Brewster when I was living in

Northern Virginia and recovering from a complicated surgery. A former university professor, she'd developed a dynamic holistic medical practice, using a style of medicine that was new to me. From India, and in the linage tradition of her country, she'd been trained as a homeopathic physician. She saved my life and opened my mind to new ways of thinking about health and wellbeing.

Over the years I've learned the power of forgiveness and learned to love and trust more completely. I've developed a positive, enthusiastic approach to life, and I want to share some of my wisdom with you. Here are my thoughts.

Honor your teachers.

I am consciously aware of my teachers, and I honor their gifts and incorporate their wisdom into my life when appropriate. Some of my best teachers are people who challenged me - people I did not want to emulate. They taught me to honor my truth and my inner strength.

Honor Universal Truth.

There are Universal Truths that show up in every religion and culture. I love the ideas presented in The Four Agreements, a classic Toltec book of wisdom by Don Miguel Ruiz.

He offers these life principles: 1. Be impeccable with your words. 2. Do not take anything personally 3. Do not make assumptions. 4. Always do your best.

Accept what is.

I've learned through personal experience that acceptance is the beginning of change. I know the more I fight against negativity, the more powerful and challenging its influence becomes. I choose to spend my time with positive thought, because my thoughts create my behavior and my life.

Monitor your thoughts and remember laughter is the best medicine.

My body, just like yours, listens and works to make my wants and needs a fact of life. If I want a positive outcome, I must think positive thoughts. Neutral thought will not lift me into robust health and wellness. Negative thought will eventually make me sick. Laughter keeps my energy flowing and lifts my mood.

Spend quiet time meditating and journaling.

These two activities, partnering with the other ideas I've mentioned, enable me to remain emotionally, energetically and physically balanced. Each morning during quiet time I have choices. I might decide on a meditative walk, a quiet introspection or feel guided to balance my energy using energy psychology or a qi gong. I end each meditation session by writing in my journal.

Honor human differences.

We are all one. I did not always understand this concept. I thought my body created a boundary and kept me separate from you and other forms of life. As an energy healer, energy psychologist and intuitive, I simply had to accept that my original belief was faulty. Energetically speaking, we are all one, yet we each have a unique life experience. My life purpose is different from yours and our differences create a beautiful human kaleidoscope. Our different beliefs and behaviors are learned. Our sameness is inborn, and is our shared humanity.

Janet Nestor, Licensed Professional Counselor, Energy Psychologist, Author and Life Enthusiast

www.mindfulpathways.com

*****

Janet's life is a glorious testimony of the power of enthusiasm.

Exercise:

7 Day Energy Module- amp up your energy. Try these exercises over the next 7 days.

Day 1-

Move your body. If you already exercise- add five minutes or add something different. If you do not exercise- move your body for 5 minutes. Talk to someone you do not know.

Day 2-

Eat at least one thing that is good for you at every meal (example- veggies- high fiber- etc) - Hydrate- drink water. Write down how much water you are drinking. Do something you have never done.

Day 3-

Close your eyes for five minutes during the day- let your mind drift and dream. Do something you fear.

Day 4-

Listen to a new piece of music. Learn some new piece of information. Write down your thoughts.

Day 5-

Turn on music and dance crazy for five minutes. Create a name for the dance you just created.

Write down 100 affirmations related to your business or career- say them out loud three times.

Day 6-

Give money to a new charity/organization- one you have not supported in the past.

Join something new (coaching program, association, club- etc). Offer support to someone (mentoring, etc).

Day 7-

Write down 200 words (at least) about shifting your energy- post this to your blog that you created in Chapter 2's exercise.

Create one new business/career objective- and write out a brief outline/plan to complete.

CHAPTER 9: LOCKING IN THE LEARNING

"Man's mind, once stretched by a new idea, never regains its original dimensions." – **Oliver Wendell Holmes**

Here we are, at the end of our journey together. Now you have the complete acronym INSPIRE and anytime you get up in the morning and you think, " I feel off today" or "this is going wrong, where can I start?" you can start by looking at the acronym and you might think, "okay, I clearly recognize that I am struggling with some of my beliefs. What new belief should I work on and what new beliefs can I bring in my life or what beliefs can I let go of?" Or you might need one of the other parts of the acronym INSPIRE.

Let's review INSPIRE –

I- is Your Compelling I-Story

N- is New Beliefs,

S- is Stepping into Inspired Action,

P- is the Three P's, People, Purpose and Prosperity.

I- is *I Love*

R- is Reaching Out

E- is Managing your Energy and Enthusiasm.

Keep this close by so you can look at the acronym, and it will help point you to an area for development and attention. The acronym INSPIRE is a tool for you to put into your toolbox to use.

Here are 4 keys for success to use as you practice the principles in this book.

1. Try something new. Choose something that has intimidated you in the past. Do something out of the norm for you. Notice the shift in energy when you do it. Do you feel a sense of accomplishment? Do you feel more confident? Do you feel capable? Do you feel energized?

2. When you set plans in place, view your plans as a promise to yourself. And keep

your promises to yourself just as you would keep a promise to someone else. Become aware of distractions so you can keep focused on your plans. Understand that some fear is natural when you try something new. Avoid procrastination. Procrastination is a habit. See yourself as empowered to put any positive habit in place. Do not see yourself as a victim of procrastination. Start on one thing...even if it is the smallest, easiest thing. That way you can build some momentum for sticking to your plans.

3. When things seem difficult, allow yourself to experience the emotions (fear, anxiety, and anger). Then work through them and get to the point where you decide that you are making it through whatever situation you are in and you have already won... Tell yourself, "I have already won; I have not given up- so I have already won."

4. Remember your past successes. Make a list of your top 100 or more successes from birth to now. Enjoy that feeling of achievement and let it fuel your progress toward your next goals.

I believe in you.

I know you can do it.

Celebrate your successes.

Be the Inspiration.

Did I say we have come to the end of our journey together? It doesn't have to be the end.

Please visit me at

www.lifeisjoyful.org or www.sherikayehoff.com

And I have a special free gift for you here:

http://www.lifeisjoyful.org/conquer.html

Sending you love, joy, abundant blessings and success.

Warmest,

Coach Sheri

ABOUT THE AUTHOR

Sheri Kaye Hoff, Ph.D. M.A., B.S., CGCL-Coach, Trainer, and Author, Sheri is a Business and Life Coach known for inspiring massive action and a catalyst for personal and business growth, joy, and profits in a way that is fun, relaxing, and fulfilling, Sheri inspires people to the do work they love and make more money. Sheri helps business owners and professionals to relax into success. She uses both spiritual and practical techniques to obliterate blocks and create dramatic change. She is a business, leadership, happiness, and inner game expert. She has overcome nearly dying, and the loss of her brother at an early age. She has made it her lifetime mission to discover the keys to happiness and success and then share them.

She is married with three children and three step-children and lives in beautiful Parker, CO.

Appendix A

Quick Meeting Tips:

I was recently asked about how to have effective work meetings...I thought...yep...people might need some quick tips on effective meetings.

Yes meetings can be a problem...and they can also be great.

Meetings are best if there is an agenda for each one...and when people go off on tangents...there is someone to say something like "Can we add that to next week's meeting...or can that be handled over email?," etc; and then gently lead the person back to the discussion at hand.

Let's say you have...a weekly sales meeting...

You could have an agenda that says (e.g.)-

- Welcome
- Status review
- Current issues (list any current things that need to be addressed)
- Upcoming events

- Long term goals (list any big projects that may need status updates)
- Training (sales techniques, etc)
- Follow up on any unfinished business.
- Assign tasks based on discussion.

I think one hour is best for most weekly meetings...possibly up to two hours depending on topics that need to be discussed. Carefully look at who needs to be at the meeting- and only have those people there.

Another thing to watch about your own meeting contributions... carefully weigh what you say... make sure all of your own contributions meet the purpose of the meeting and are not "devil's advocate" type of contributions. Yes, logic and questioning are important, but not every issue requires an exhaustive analysis. Many people fall into a devil's advocate role and this eats up time and is not very productive.

If you are holding the meeting...stick to your agenda...and keep it moving along.

These tips also work for other types of meetings (masterminds, fundraising, etc).

Cheers to all your productive meetings!

Appendix B

Money Goals:

Set some money goals- be brave and courageous.

Keep your daily goals in front of you each day.

Record income from every source.

Do the happy dance every time you get any money in.

Every time take money in or send money out - visually imagine that you are receiving back ten times (or one hundred times that amount). For example, you pay the water bill of $150- as you write the check (and bless it) imagine that $1500 or $15000 is coming back to you. This keeps you away from the feeling of not having enough.

Another tip for paying bills is to pay something over the minimum amount- even if it is one dollar.

Avoid having any negative conversations about your money or anyone else's money.

See everyone as blessed and prospered.

When you give money to a charity or anyone-see this as not that you are meeting a need-see it as you are blessing their prosperity.

Give generously with a prosperous and blessed attitude.

Use positive affirmations.

Be Bold -Think BIG.

If you own a business- have money goals that are separate from the biz goals.

Learn how to feel great about money all of the time.

- Money goal for this year:
- Money goal for next year:
- Money goal in five years:
- Money goal in ten years:
- Daily goal:
- Weekly goal:
- Monthly goal:

Appendix C

Leadership Log:

Use the below prompts to track your leadership behavior for one week...

- I acted like a leader when I ....
- I inspired someone else when...
- _____inspired me when he or she...
- I inspired myself when I ...

Reflections...What shows up for me as I look at my answers? How do I get inspired? How do I inspire others? Is a system apparent that I could replicate? Do I notice things I want to change?

Excerpt from Keys to Living Joyfully

By Sheri Kaye Hoff

Is Your Heart Thinking Right?

These are such simple words, yet the meaning is profound.
Whatever you think about and internalize in your heart, is what you become. Whatever you believe in your core or spirit is what you become. So if you believe that you are incapable of joy and happiness, this belief will manifest in your life. If you are worried about your weight, your bills, never having enough money, being sick, losing your job and the list could go on and on, this is what you have created in your life.

As humans, we may think we have little control over many or even most things in the world around us, but we do have the ability to control our thoughts. Reality is created for you in your thoughts. There have been many times when the disaster you created in your mind was far worse than the actual circumstances, yet you experienced the horror of your thoughts. Think of it this way:

You sense that something is wrong at work and you start to worry, people at work start acting differently towards you because you have changed. This difference then heightens your sense of insecurity, which further alters your thoughts and your actions. Ultimately, work becomes a miserable place, which you have brought on YOURSELF.

If you are actively engaging in this type of self-sabotage, forgive yourself and then act on your new sense of the importance of thoughts. No good will come out of berating yourself for past actions. Now that you know that your thoughts create reality, you can act to correct negative patterns.

You may be saying to yourself that you cannot control your thoughts. You may even be saying that thoughts just happen. You can change your thoughts. Knowing this gives you deep power. What are you thinking about you right now? Are you thinking about all of the things you should be doing? Are you worrying about today? Or tomorrow? Are you angry with people who have hurt you? You can be free from all of these thoughts and it is a conscious choice of freedom.

When my oldest daughter was in 7th grade, she became chronically ill and missed 25 days of school. She had lived most of her school years as a successful "A" and "B" student. Suddenly, she was earning "C"s and even an occasional "D". She started to buy in to the "fact" that she was not a good scholar or student. She started to believe that she was not smart. She thought these things instead of seeing the reality that missing school impacts learning and grades. She had surgery at the end of 7th grade and became much healthier. However, her grades were still suffering at the beginning of 8th grade because she no longer believed that she was a good student.

Her turning point came when I realized all of the negative thoughts that she was spinning in her head.

We talked about this and created some affirmations like:

"I am so thankful that I remember everything I study"

"I am so thankful that I am great at taking tests"

"I am so thankful that I remember to bring all of my assignments to school and turn them in on time".
Gradually, she internalized a new view of herself as a smart, capable student, and her grades started coming back up again.

Think about this situation and apply it to your own life. Where are you struggling? Are you struggling financially? Is it hard to maintain a healthy weight? Are you unhappy and depressed? Is it a chore for you to wake up and begin each day? Are your interpersonal relationships difficult? Think about how you think about these things. This is a gift we have as human beings—the fact that we can think about our thinking.

If you truly wrap your arms around this idea of how we shape our lives based on our thoughts, you hold the key to unlocking amazing transformative power in your life. In my own life, I experienced the tragic suicide death of my younger brother when I was 17 years old and he was 15 years old. Of course, this altered my life forever. One of the most harmful long-term effects on my life was how I viewed my ability to experience happiness. This loss in my life is what eventually inspired my quest of determining how a person could live a joyful life.

Since I experienced such extreme grief and shock, I was naturally depressed and in therapy for a few years after the death of my brother. Even after I finished therapy, my outlook on my life seemed permanently altered. I believed that true happiness did not exist for me. I began a cycle of on and off depression that influenced my life for the next twenty years. As I entered my late thirties, I thought of myself as a depressed person and even tried to reach acceptance of this in my life. Then, I realized that I could not, would not accept that happiness would be forever elusive to me.

I have always believed intellectually in positive thinking. I viewed it as something that I needed to "psych myself up to do" and I did not have the energy to do it. I also most often acted positively and came across to others as an enthusiastic outgoing person even though I felt miserable on the inside. I craved being able to feel peaceful and content. In my heart, I doubted whether positive thinking could permanently alter habits of thoughts that existed for years.

One day the light bulb went on for me. I came to view that thinking could be disciplined just like actions. I learned that I could methodically reprogram my thinking and live the life that I always dreamed of living—a life of joy, peace, passion, and energy every moment of the day.

This is how I reprogrammed my mind. Every time I caught myself dwelling on the negative. I would declare aloud:

"I am so thankful that I am so happy".

At first, I felt silly, but I refused to allow negative thoughts to simmer. I took responsibility for my thoughts. Any time I found myself getting sucked into despair and worry, I reminded myself that this was a choice I was making and I wanted to choose good for my life.
A simple example of this is when I was stuck in rush-hour traffic and felt the anxiety rising in my mind. Instead of letting this stress and anxiety take over, I would calmly say,

"Thank you that I have all of the time I need to arrive at my destination".

I felt immediate calm and it seemed that almost every time, a way out or forward would open for me.

Rush-hour traffic is a small example and may not seem significant to you, but what it did for me is prove that the technique works. When I realized that this was working on a small level in my life, the possibility opened for me that this simple process could profoundly change my whole life in a huge way.

When I knew that I would have to handle a difficult situation at work, I would say:

"Thank you for my perfectly smooth meeting and positive results."

If I felt upset with my husband or children, instead of letting those feelings fester and grow, I would say:

"Thank you for my great relationships with my family."

I truly stopped being irritated by small things and most big things. I began to feel a sense of calm and peace. Joy began seeping into my life as I made some room to experience it.

I began to keep a daily journal of my affirmations. Now, I have the ability to go through past journals and see how my life has changed.

Do you struggle with your finances? For much of my adult life, I have been plagued with money worries and concerns. For my entire married life, my husband has been self-employed. For those of you who are small business owners, you know that cash flow can be unpredictable. Even when things were fine, I had this fear that there was never going to be enough money to pay the bills or get ahead financially. I worked full time, as well.

Our lives together were completely immersed in my husband working long hours at his business, I worked full time, and we were raising our three children. Life was a constant scheduling challenge and the area that suffered for me was my health (lack of sleep and lack of exercise).

Looking back, most of my fears were unrealized. Yes, there were times that bills were paid a little late, but we made it. Focusing on fear and worry was a waste of my time and a complete drain on my spirit. I started to apply my thought reprogramming process to our financial lives.

I am a very spiritual person and a Christian. My faith is vital to my life and is probably the only thing that truly made me survive the crushing experience of losing my brother. In my darkest times when I was angry with God, sometimes I could only utter the words:

"Please, God, Please, God".

My affirmations, prayers, and meditations are based on my faith and belief in God. However, affirmations still work even if you are not sure what role religion and God play in your life. Below is the plan that I created to keep my thoughts heading in the right direction. Please feel free to adapt the method to what works for you.

I thanked God every day for financial abundance, and I praised and blessed everything in my life. As soon as I began to think about worrying about a bill, I thanked God for the company where we owed money, and I praised and blessed that company. I praised and blessed my husband's business and his customers.

Within three months of doing this, my husband's business was taking in new clients. He experienced unusual growth. I was able to leave my job and take a job teaching at a college where I worked from home when I was not physically in class teaching. I also taught some of my classes online. This freed me to pursue my doctoral studies and to pursue my passion for writing.

My life started to turn into my dream life. The life-changing piece of this is that if I had my previous attitude, I might not have recognized that I was truly beginning to live my dream life. I would have been stuck in my previous worry pattern of fearing the worst.

I know it sounds unbelievable, but controlling your thoughts completely alters the fabric and substance of your life.

"Man, alone, has the power to transform his thoughts into physical reality; man, alone, can dream and make his dreams come true."
Napoleon Hill

Kathryn's Comments:

"I loved taking part in Sheri Kaye Hoff's Be the Inspiration Leadership Program and continue to draw upon what I learned and the benefits of this experience. Sheri put so much into this program and it is packed with tools and techniques that I continue to use. Sheri included recordings, coaching, handouts, and more to provide a complete experience. Having the recordings and handouts helps me to integrate what I have learned and go deeper into the concepts, even after the conclusion of the program.

What I learned about leadership has supported me in all of my roles, professionally and personally. Sheri helped me to get comfortable with embracing my personal story and the value it brings. Writing my I-story was healing and powerful. Sheri is truly a role model for me, demonstrating that great joy can come through inspiring others.

Sheri's coaching saved me valuable time by pointing me in the right direction. Her warmth, encouragement, and guidance moved me into action, and I took steps and moved forward rather than staying stuck in confusion or overwhelm. Through her program, I

*clarified my message and gained the
confidence to step into a new leadership role.
She helped me to find my voice.*

*Sheri had a keen intuitive sense for what
participants in the program were
experiencing, and she took the time to address
those concerns as they arose. I was comforted
to know the challenges were common among
the participants and anyone stretching beyond
his or her comfort zone. With Sheri's gentle
support, I felt energized and inspired
throughout this experience.*

*I am excited to be bringing this fresh energy
into my work as a literacy interventionist in a
public school and as a Family Manager Coach
helping moms to maximize time, energy, and
peace of mind. I would highly recommend this
program to individuals looking for this
enrichment in their own lives and am
confident that through Sheri's coaching they
can achieve great results, too."*

Kathryn Quintana, Certified Family Manager
Coach

http://www.simplesolutionsorganizing.com/

Books by Sheri Kaye Hoff available in paperback and kindle editions.

Keys to Living Joyfully

Living Successfully and Joyfully Everyday: 90 Days of Inspiration

Top Life Coaching Tips: Live each Day with more Peace, Passion, Energy, and Joy.

Be the Inspiration: 7 Ways to Inspire Your World

Relax Into Inspired Action: Connect the Pieces and Live Fulfilled

For book orders go to:

Amazon.com

Barnes and Noble

www.sherikayehoff.com